babystrology

* The Astrological Guide to Your Little Star *

JUDI VITALE, Astrology Researcher for *Marie Claire*

Aadamsmedia

Avon, Massachusetts

Published by
Adams Media, a division of F+W Media, Inc.
57 Littlefield Street, Avon, MA 02322. U.S.A.
www.adamsmedia.com

ISBN 10: 1-4405-3888-3
ISBN 13: 978-1-4405-3888-9
eISBN 10: 1-4405-4017-9
eISBN 13: 978-1-4405-4017-2

Printed in the United States of America.

10   9   8   7   6   5   4   3   2   1

Library of Congress Cataloging-in-Publication Data
is available from the publisher.

This publication is designed to provide accurate and authoritative information with regard to the subject matter covered. It is sold with the understanding that the publisher is not engaged in rendering legal, accounting, or other professional advice. If legal advice or other expert assistance is required, the services of a competent professional person should be sought.

—From a *Declaration of Principles* jointly adopted by a Committee of the American Bar Association and a Committee of Publishers and Associations

Many of the designations used by manufacturers and sellers to distinguish their product are claimed as trademarks. Where those designations appear in this book and Adams Media was aware of a trademark claim, the designations have been printed with initial capital letters.

Art © istockphoto/LokFung/browndogstudios/andrewshka and © 123rf/Shen En-Min.

This book is available at quantity discounts for bulk purchases.
For information, please call 1-800-289-0963.

Dedication

This book is dedicated to my son, David, who has brought me joy from the day he came into being, by teaching me that in all my life my greatest purpose and privilege has been—and is—being his mom.

Acknowledgments

No one person makes a book, not even the author. I am deeply grateful for the support of my agent, Holly Schmidt; the quick-thinking and capable editors and publishers who entrusted me with this precious project; and my family and friends who understood when I couldn't go places and do things with them while I was engaged in the joyful labor of writing this book. Also, the teachers and clients who have nurtured and educated me in astrology and the art of writing about it get extra hugs for helping me to deepen my knowledge and broaden my love and compassion for all "babies"—no matter what sign we might be.

CONTENTS

Introduction

When a child is born, who they are is a great unknown. What will make him smile? What will be her favorite color? Will he grow up to love books, make friends easily, become passionate about the great outdoors? Will she love the same things that you love? How can you best nurture the tiny little one that's landed in your care and help him to grow into a confident, caring, personable person?

It's difficult to know how to provide for the emotional life of a child when you haven't yet learned who that child really is. But knowing—and nurturing—the person that your child really is deep inside can make all the difference in the world. Fortunately, you already know the most important thing you need to know about your little one: his sun sign! Here you'll learn how to use babystrology—the astrology of your baby—to discover how certain personality traits and proclivities will pay into your child's development. Whether your little one has the soft temperament of a Pisces, the confidence of a Leo, or the loving nature of a Cancer you'll learn how to ensure that you're giving him what he needs, whether it's plenty of time in your arms, a beautifully decorated nursery or bedroom, or playing a game that engages his passions. You'll also learn what songs to sing to your Aries, what books your Scorpio will love, and what special talents you can nurture in your little Capricorn.

But if you're a Virgo, how can you relate to a sweet, little Gemini? How can a Libra parent a Pisces? In each chapter, after you learn what to expect from a child with your baby's sign, you'll be able to see how someone of your sign will be able to relate and you'll get an idea of what joys—and what challenges—the mix of your signs will bring. So get ready to learn more about your little one, yourself, and how the relationship you'll share has been written in the stars. Enjoy!

How to Use This Book

A strology is an ancient practice, and it's based on the way the planets, the sun, and the moon are placed in the sky when a person is born. While the complete reading of a person's astrology is quite complex, you only need to know the basics to gain some insight into the personality and inner life of your child. To do this, you need your child's sun sign, which is determined by the zodiac sign the sun is in at the time of birth. Find your child's sign on the chart below:

DATES	SUN SIGN
March 21–April 20	Aries
April 21–May 20	Taurus
May 21–June 20	Gemini
June 21–July 21	Cancer
July 22–August 21	Leo
August 22–September 20	Virgo
September 21–October 21	Libra
October 22–November 21	Scorpio
November 22–December 20	Sagittarius
December 21–January 20	Capricorn
January 21–February 20	Aquarius
February 21–March 20	Pisces

Note: Some people believe that a person can share the characteristics of two sun signs, which is called being "on the cusp." However, when a baby is born, the sun is in one zodiac sign or another. If your child's birthday falls within a few days of two signs, you should either have the full birth chart calculated by an astrologer, using the date, time of day, and place of the birth or you should take a look at the descriptions of the signs to see which one seems to fit. Whether you use calculation or instinct, pick a sun sign and stick to it; you'll be connecting with your child in a way you never thought possible before you know it.

✳ SOME TERMS TO UNDERSTAND ✳

This book will be more fun to read if you know a little bit of astrology lingo. You won't have to take a tutorial, but knowing the basic meaning of a few terms you'll read throughout the book will be a huge help:

RULING PLANET: Each sign has an association with the sun, the moon, or one of the planets. This planet helps to create the atmosphere of that zodiac sign and shapes the character of the people born under it.

EXALTED PLANET: Some planets have "second homes" in other sun signs, where they can function well or in harmony with their basic nature. When a planet is in a sign it feels comfortable in, we say it's in "exaltation."

SIGN CLASSIFICATIONS

It's also important to know that the signs are classified by *element*, which in astrology's view can be fire, earth, air, or water. Elements help shape the "personalities" of the signs, and the people born under them. They are classified this way to reflect the ancient view of the four major means of manifestation. The organization of these signs is as follows:

FIRE SIGNS:
(ARIES, LEO, AND SAGITTARIUS)

These people are active and forceful. You always know when they're in the room!

EARTH SIGNS:
(TAURUS, VIRGO, AND CAPRICORN)

These individuals are practical, comparatively calm, and resourceful. They really know how to make their ideas manifest into material rewards.

AIR SIGNS:
(GEMINI, LIBRA, AND AQUARIUS)

Mental acuity is the telling characteristic of the human beings born under this sign. They think their way out of situations quickly and always come up with rational explanations for the experiences they have in life.

WATER SIGNS:
(CANCER, SCORPIO, AND PISCES)

Ruled by the emotions, the people born under these signs are sensitive and empathic. They also tend to have very strong instincts and can anticipate the needs and desires of others, perhaps before their friends, relatives, cohorts, and colleagues even know they have them!

The signs are also divided up by *mode*, which can be cardinal, fixed, or mutable. This way of dividing the signs is based upon where they fall with regard to each season (winter, spring, summer, fall), as in the first, second, or third portion of the season. The modes of the signs are as follows:

CARDINAL SIGNS:
(ARIES, CANCER, LIBRA, AND CAPRICORN)

Cardinal signs like to start activities the same way they bring the start of each season. They may not be so great at finishing them, though!

FIXED SIGNS:
(TAURUS, LEO, SCORPIO, AND AQUARIUS):

Creatures of habit, the fixed signs would rather keep things the way they are. They are great at finishing projects, but they sometimes struggle with the part about moving on!

MUTABLE SIGNS:
(GEMINI, VIRGO, SAGITTARIUS, AND PISCES)

These signs are easy-going and will roll with the punches, but they often struggle with skills or projects that require organization.

Now that you know the basics of your child's sign, it's time to take a closer look. Read on to learn more about the hidden personality, challenges, and passions of your precious little one.

CHAPTER 1

Aries:

The Wild Ram

BORN BETWEEN:	March 21–April 20
RULING PLANET:	Mars – The warlike, aggressive side
EXALTED PLANET:	The Sun
COLOR:	Red. Bright Red!
GEMSTONES:	Diamond and Clear Quartz

YOUR LITTLE ARIES BURST ON TO THE SCENE at the same time spring came to wake up the world. From now on, this child will figure that arousing the rest of us is pretty much his job. Aries is a *fire* sign, and because it's the first sign of spring, it's also *cardinal*. Aries is intelligent and crafty, but most of the activity going on in Aries's being stems from physical activity. From the beginning you'll notice that your little Aries is very forceful, and willful, too. Strong, energetic, and courageous, the Aries child wants to push through to new frontiers . . . constantly!

Aries is in almost constant motion. If you don't give this child enough stimulation, she will demand it, most likely by crying, kicking, and thrashing fists. When she's too small to walk, try to calm her down with lots of walks and rides. However, you must avoid allowing Aries to believe you're going to cater to every whim and wish. This little one is always pushing the envelope, and will constantly try to make you go where no parent has gone before!

Aries children are also doers. They don't like to talk about playing a game; they want to pick up the ball and get in on the action. Aries experiences everything through physical sensation, and although not the cuddliest baby, your Aries child will from time to time seek the comfort of being held—just not too tightly! On some level, your child will look for nonverbal clues to check in with you and see if you've lost *all* your patience yet. Just don't expect your little ram to be very sympathetic when you have a bad day; Aries has very little sensitivity and doesn't consider your feelings, because he has trouble seeing beyond the concept of "I am." When Aries gets angry, it's usually because her freedom has been restricted. Those months where baby is crawling and toddling and unable to understand the difference between danger and adventure can be very trying for the parent of the Aries, yet the reward of seeing this strong and tireless soul through first steps and big falls is well worth the effort.

* YOUR ARIES BOY *

Most little boys will seem to have more curiosity and energy than the average girl, but your Aries boy will definitely stand out as the embodiment of constant action. He needs a large amount of physical activity, adequate attention, and most of all, your patience. Be an advocate for your Aries boy. Don't let teachers or other caregivers single him out for refusing to be passive and agreeable at all times. Supplement organized activities with extracurricular opportunities to run, play, and explore!

The Aries boy won't be very tolerant about waiting, and he'll need to be taught about taking his turn. It's in his basic nature to run to the head of the line and be "first," and there will be times when he bowls over less-assertive children, or at least pushes them aside. He feels a responsibility to be the one who's out ahead of the pack, scouting out danger (and dabbling in adventure). Keep an eye on him because he can move through a crowd like a knife moves through butter.

Your Aries boy also has a very big fascination with violence, and even gore. Many Aries boys grow up to be fine surgeons because they are fearless and somewhat detached from the more squeamish reactions people have to seeing blood or needles. Others make fine law enforcement officials or soldiers. All are interested in TV shows, games, and activities that exhibit aggression. This can be healthy to a point, but in a world where some video games are more realistic than most of us can stomach, it might be wise to give your Aries boy some extra exercise and some idea of his own ability to hurt and be hurt through the study of martial arts. In a safe and protected environment, he can learn how to fight so he can satisfy his hunger to protect and defend those who matter most to him, without damaging his body or his psyche.

YOUR ARIES GIRL

Before you try to dress her up in frilly lace and put fussy bows in her hair, you need to recognize who this strong young lady is! Aries girls might not be as quiet and sweet-seeming as most, but they are very loyal, loving, and protective of you and everyone who is dear to them. Your Aries girl needs nurturing, but she also requires enough freedom to be the live wire she really is.

This little girl may be rough and temperamental when she feels as though she's being restricted. She might kick her way out of the swaddling blanket or throw toys when she's mad. Aries girls aren't afraid to get dirty, and they will often rather play with more active boys than sit calmly at the tea party with their fellow females. Among all-girl groups, your daughter is likely to quickly emerge as the alpha female. There's just something about her that's stronger, braver, and more confident than the others that surround her, and they recognize this immediately. Aries women are the kinds who don't believe in barriers set up by gender. They're the ones who become pilots and pioneers. They love nature and enjoy entertainment that some of their female peers may shun as being "just for boys."

It's important to allow your Aries to exercise her "inner male" and not be concerned about whether she fits in with other girls. She probably doesn't want to fit in with anyone! She just wants to get as much adventure, excitement, and fun as she can fit into any given day.

When it comes to clothes, forcing ultra-feminine colors won't do, either. Aries will choose her own style, and comfort will come far ahead of fashion! Even after you spend a half-hour making her hair look perfect, she'll walk away from you and pull out the barrettes, bands, and bows so she can be more at ease.

Give your Aries girl more of what she wants, within reason. Let her try her hand at sports, even if it means she's the only girl on the team. (She won't even notice!) Eventually, she'll grow to be as feminine as any woman, but she'll also possess the charm of being strong, dynamic, and nearly indestructible!

✳ TALENTS AND AFFINITIES ✳

SPORTS

Aries has an incredible amount of physical energy, and whether you help your child channel it into useful activity or not, it will come out! Aries is competitive, but not in a malicious, nasty way. Physical domination is a thing with Aries, whether male or female. For this reason, your little ram may grow to love karate or gymnastics more than soccer or tennis.

LANGUAGE

Verbal communication might come fast and furiously, or if your baby gets exceptionally frustrated, it will take a while. Aries are more than capable of making themselves understood without words, as you'll find out when your tot drags you across the room to reach a favorite toy or get a snack. To encourage this child's language skills you may need to play games by making your little Aries say the word before you retrieve the desired object, but prepare for some resistance!

LEADERSHIP

You'll never have to worry about your Aries child running off to be like anyone else, and that includes you. Aries is a true, natural-born leader, and will not only march to the beat of a different drummer, but come up with a whole new rhythm! Other children will tend to follow your Aries child, so it's important to instill positive goals and good intentions at the earliest age possible.

LITTLE CHALLENGES

Almost from the beginning, you'll notice that your little Aries is a "handful." The squirming, kicking, thrashing, and yelling you'll see in your infant is completely normal. Your baby is a bundle of physical energy, and must at all times have useful, productive ways to discharge it. You'll know your Aries child needs to run around the room a few times when that legendary temper flares. Deprived from something this little Aries wants, he may explode emotionally, and if you're lucky, only verbally. Aries children are the ones voted most likely to hurl a building block across the room at another child—or you—when provoked; but lucky for everyone involved, Aries explodes and then quickly forgets what was so maddening. Obviously, Aries will have to learn to control that temper, and that job will be up to you.

DISCIPLINE

Strict, consistent, and absolute boundaries are the best thing you can offer your Aries child; after all, once your little one learns to act in a way that's acceptable to you and the rest of society, he can be left to develop all that independence and strident, spirited leadership. Aries is the child who doesn't seem to hear you when you say, "Don't touch," so you will have to say it loudly. Within limits, you can let "natural consequences" take over, but no matter how many times you said you'd never do it, there will be times when you must physically remove your child from hazards such as fire, falls, and other types of bodily harm. The best way to show Aries you are displeased is to restrict his motion. Start by confining your tot to his crib or room. You'll want to monitor the situation closely, of course, but expect to hear screaming, banging, and crying. Still, no matter how raucous it gets in there, Aries shouldn't be allowed to come back out until he is calm, relaxed, and apologetic.

FAVORITE THINGS

SING THESE SONGS WITH YOUR ARIES CHILD

> **"Pony Boy/Girl":** The bouncing, "giddyap" part is crucial.

> **"Yankee Doodle":** Every Aries loves to march!

> **"Ring Around the Rosie":** This "all fall down" action song is a sure-fire Aries crowd pleaser.

WATCH MOVIES LIKE THIS WITH YOUR ARIES CHILD

> *Peter Pan:* Swashbuckling and staying up all night—Aries is there.

> *Kung Fu Panda:* Aries can witness the miracle of overcoming obstacles and achieving heady goals—not to mention the top-notch kung-fu action.

> *The Land Before Time:* A charming, uplifting tale of overcoming fear with courage and leadership.

PLAY THESE GAMES WITH YOUR ARIES CHILD

> **Follow the Leader:** You might start out playing top dog, but before long, Aries will take over!

> **Tag:** Aries will love to run away from you, but won't love the idea of being "it."

> **Pirates:** Even Aries girls will adore dressing up and acting tough.

READ THESE BOOKS, RHYMES, AND FAIRY TALES TO YOUR ARIES CHILD

> **"The Labors of Hercules":** Stories of fighting off nasty creatures with heroic passion will keep Aries enthralled and inspired.

> **"Jack Be Nimble":** An action ditty with a lesson about burning one's toe built right in.

> **"Jack and the Beanstalk":** Giant slaying? Just one of Aries's many ambitions.

TREAT YOUR ARIES CHILD TO THESE FOODS

> **Beef:** Meaty, delicious and a real energy producer.

> **Tomato juice:** Yes, really! Aries likes the color and the tangy taste.

> **Bananas:** High in potassium, and tasty too.

Note: Aries children eat the same way they do everything else: fast and voraciously. They like protein-rich foods, and will often eat on the run.

ARIES'S BABY STYLE

Simple, but with a taste for bright colors, Aries is extremely expressive and that curiosity leads to a lot of grass and mud stains. Avoid pastels and clothes that rip and tear easily.

GIRLS: She'll eschew the princess accessories and ballerina tutu for stretch pants and a sturdy pair of kicks.

BOYS: He'll choose the red shirt over the white one you want him to wear to a special occasion. He wants to make it easier for everyone to find him!

ARIES'S ENVIRONMENT

When you recognize just how active (and tiring!) your little Aries can be, you might start bringing "cooling" colors such as blue and purple into the nursery, but hold off before you invest too much. Bright colors such as red, orange, and hot pink cancel out some of Aries's fire.

CALMING ARIES

Aries children cry more than most, and you'll soon discover that the tears start to flow when Aries perceives he isn't being noticed. Aries will cry for all sorts of reasons, so you have to be very sensitive to the variations in the tone. The hunger and discomfort ones will be more fervent, and you'll learn to respond promptly. Sometimes Aries can get headaches—because this is the part of your little ram's horns-first body that is most sensitive—or often needs to be calmed just because he is upset from not getting what he wants. In these cases, gently rub Aries's head, and before long the thrashing and wailing will end.

The best way to get Aries ready to go to sleep is to tire this ram out. In infancy, you can achieve this by letting baby kick and giggle, and later on, with regular exercise. You'll find that, once in while, this child will just have to run around the block.

STIMULATING ARIES

Aries children might seem to be over-stimulated, but don't misread what they really need from you. Your little one needs you to provide activities that help channel that impulsive energy and develop a longer attention span. Try these toys:

- **Sports Equipment:** Start with the baby gym and go from there.
- **A Pith Helmet:** Good for inspiring adventures—and protecting that butting ram's head!
- **Modeling Clay:** Even if your child isn't a sculptor, punching, molding, and forming will demonstrate the art of being productive.

ARIES'S LEARNING STYLE

Aries learns by doing, which is why this child is always touching what mustn't be touched, and trying to do things (such as walk or crawl before it's humanly possible) on his own. Take your little Aries to museums and other exhibits that are "hands-on," and if there's some running folded into the activity, all the better! Strive to find teachers who understand active children like yours, and teach them by directing that energy rather than trying to suppress it.

PARENTING ARIES

If your sign is . . .

ARIES

It's a gift to get a baby who's the same sign you are, but don't forget what's most important about being an Aries—independence and individuality. As demanding as you know you are, your baby might seem to be even more so. Your child will constantly preface sentences with, "I want . . . " Your relatives will wonder if there's room enough for two fierce personalities like yours in the same household, but you'll get the last laugh by enjoying every moment you share with this wonderful child. In the meantime, you have to grow up and raise your baby at the same time. Your main job is to teach your ram that the world doesn't really revolve around little Aries.

Your child needs to learn these lessons early, so practice social integration by introducing your little one to the exercise of fitting into groups at an early age. A baby exercise class or play group for your older child will give both you and your little ram the chance to find a place to shine, but also an opportunity to share the joys of cooperation and friendship. Then, you can *both* go out for ice cream.

TAURUS

The proud parent in you will be overwhelmed with love when you meet your Aries baby, but by the time you bring your excitable bundle of joy home, you could get a little scared. How are you supposed to keep the calm and quiet of your universe with an Aries in the house? The secret is to bring out your own "beasty" side. When you find your little ram challenging, you must respond with tactics that cancel out Aries's agenda. By being stubborn and unyielding about maintaining your house rules, you might not become best pals with your Aries child, but you'll be the kind of parent that your ram will respect and look up to with love.

When Aries's temper flares, don't respond in kind. Show your child that it's okay to be angry, but talking about it or working it out another way is far more productive than throwing tantrums. Despite your less-than-eager attitude toward physical activity, encouraging your Aries to be more active might improve your health, too. Show Aries how to develop talents and work with passion, so one day this feisty little tyke can channel all that outpouring force into a successful and prosperous career.

GEMINI

Before you even put your little Aries into bed for the first time, you need to know that there are no words that will magically make this baby behave and become a clever conversationalist while still in nursery school. You'll learn from this little ram that there's life outside your circle of friends, and by watching this baby discover the world, day by day, you can learn to appreciate the value of primitive, physical sensations. You'll also have to develop your own attention span to a greater degree, and ensure that you're really "minding" the child. This child can get in trouble faster than you can work a room, so always have at least one eye on him, and stay within range so you can step in before there's a date with trouble.

When your little Aries won't settle down, you can use your natural talents at trickery to provide distractions. Your entertaining style will engage Aries and allow you to take the focus off whatever's bothering your child and on to the funny thing you're doing with a napkin or a nearby nose. You and this ram both need to develop a more sustained attention span, so play memory games or have spelling "contests." By appreciating your differences, you can both learn a lot of great lessons as you help this adorably dynamic baby grow up.

CANCER

For you, an Aries child might be the most exciting of them all. This bundle of energy will tire you out, and you'll constantly wish that Aries could be more patient, but the sheer love of life that this child demonstrates on a daily basis is enough to make your heart melt. Yet, there will be things about your Aries baby that you may not expect when you dish out your huge helpings of unconditional love on this tot.

Aries likes the comfort and cuddling you provide, but won't want it all of the time. You might sense that your child wants to break free of you, and acts as though she is being held down and restrained when all you want to do is show your affection.

This need to be free to go wherever and whenever is part of the constitution of all those born under the sign of the ram, but obviously, it should only be satisfied within limits. You'll have to find a way of allowing your Aries to roam without exposing him to an undue amount of danger. Also, don't let your feelings get hurt if Aries pushes you away. This child appreciates your efforts, especially when you understand that need to be free.

LEO

You'll walk around for weeks with a puffed-out chest and a permanent smile when you meet your Aries baby. This alert, active, and bubbly child will seem like a clone of you, at least at first. You and Aries do share many traits in common: you're both outgoing, super-friendly, and you both like to lead—which is where problems could begin to develop!

You might be used to people looking to you for direction and encouragement, but Aries thinks you're the one who should be doing the following! Even as a young infant, this little ram will question your authority and show stunning assertions of pure will; for example, you might see this as Aries squirms, kicks, and squeals until you alter the feeding position to the precise way your very self-assertive infant finds most comfortable. You could be strict and stern but this won't get you the best results. To get Aries to live within safe and healthy boundaries, you'll have to demonstrate who the "real" boss is, but with every appreciation for your child's unruly, yet admirable, spirit. Get involved in activities that you and your little ram can do together that show off your superior strength and skill. You will gain your child's deference when you demonstrate your potential to show leadership and mastery. Throw a ball back and forth, or take Aries to the pool for swim lessons. Let your child try to run faster and jump higher, but let it be known that when he falls, you'll be there to save the day. Respect will follow.

VIRGO

You might think you have parenting this new member of the family all mapped out—from diapers to doctoral degree—but your Aries child will make sure things don't work out the way you planned! The unpredictable and pulsating energy of little Aries will always keep you jumping. This ram's adventurous streak will be at the root of close brushes with injury and many messes to clean up. Can you be related to this child?

While you care about the details, Aries can't be bothered with them. You prefer neatness and order, but Aries tends to throw belongings wherever they will land. The little baby you hoped to swaddle and read to can't stand to be tied down, and will wear you out physically as well as mentally as you strive to keep him busy and contented. There is one thing you can do to make this task easier, and that is to loosen up. You might not be able to keep your house the way you'd like, or pin Aries down to a tight and orderly schedule, but by opening your heart and learning to laugh more, you'll get the biggest kick you can imagine just watching this bright, assertive, and adventurous child grow.

LIBRA

You might not always see things the way your Aries does, but the two of you have a lot to learn from one another. You might sense this immediately when you first hold this rather strong and active infant. Aries represents pure will, and while you understand this concept, you might have trouble engaging in the arguments required to rise to the responsibility of containing it.

You're going to have to get used to things not being peaceful all of the time. Aries will make noise and cause excitement, because without these things it's hard for Aries to feel alive. Of course you'll have to make sure your living space is set up to protect Aries from her own misadventures, but it's very important that you don't disapprove of everything your baby does. Your little ram needs your support.

Aries stays a baby for a very long time, often into adulthood. While you are more centered on other people, Aries has a "me first" attitude that isn't always appropriate. Encourage Aries to grow out of this by showing how comforting it is to have a best friend, and later in life, a partner who you can rely on to be there for you, always.

SCORPIO

On lots of levels, you and your little Aries will understand each other, but there will also be times when you may become frustrated. Far from being malleable and easy to console like other babies are, your Aries child is startlingly independent. On one hand, you'll dislike it when you find it impossible to control your child; but on the other, you'll admire this independent streak.

You'll have to set firm limits for your little ram, though, and as a Scorpio you're more than capable of enforcing them. In fact, it could that be your little Aries was sent to you for the sole purpose of learning how to color within the lines, both literally and figuratively. Encourage physical activity, but try to get it so it's done within structures. Neither you nor your child really like playing by the rules, but it's your job to be the parent and teach your lively Aries why it's so important to know what the rules are and what they mean. Dole out your disapproval in small doses, and don't try to quash your Aries child's will. Containing Aries energy within a healthy structure is a good idea, but constraining it could be a big mistake!

SAGITTARIUS

You'll love your Aries's extra energy from the beginning. Just like you, this tiny child displays enthusiasm and vigor that goes beyond what most people consider "normal." It's fun to have a child who keeps up with you when it comes to physical stamina and emotional intensity. Before you get too cozy, though, you need to know a few things about this fun-to-be-with child.

Aries will struggle to gain dominance over you from the beginning by playing on your desire to please; your little ram may do this by seeing how often you will come when cried for, but you can't let that happen. Although you'd like to be seen as the "nice" or "cool" parent, you'll have to put your foot down with Aries from time to time. Show Aries what it means to be "fair," even when it might require you to be *un*-fair with your stubbornly territorial tyke. Aries children need to experience consequences directly, so if your child gets pushy, show what happens when you push back! If you teach your little ram how to get along with other people by adopting a "live and let live" attitude, you'll be doing the most wonderful thing possible for your delightfully dynamic Aries.

CAPRICORN

While you may think you're the boss, your Aries child might have another idea. While you certainly will be able to keep this baby from running your life without much trouble at all, you'll be amused at the dominant personality of your little tyke; there's something about the Aries baby, with all the crying spells and tantrums, you find enticing. But while you totally understand where your little one is coming from, you also know how important it will be for your child to learn how to survive *with* the world as well as in spite of it.

You're far too smart to surmise you can simply tell a child with this kind of strong spirit what to do and expect your wishes will be instantly honored. You'll instinctively know how to reward Aries for the things that are done well and ignore him when he deliberately misbehaves. This is probably the worst thing you can do to someone who is so self-centered, so don't be too cruel about it. Yet by making Aries wait for your approval, you're teaching a most valuable lesson—the joy and satisfaction of delayed gratification.

AQUARIUS

You and your Aries come from two very different worlds, but with the right amount of work, you can come to share some very pleasant common ground. The first thing you'll notice about your Aries baby will be her physically oriented way of experiencing the world. This baby must touch things in order to know what they are, and this will frustrate you; particularly if your little one puts one of your precious collectibles in danger of being smashed!

Aries will probably never be as cerebral as you, but that doesn't mean that your child isn't smart. You'll realize that when you see how quickly this child can figure out how to undo that snazzy "childproof" lock you put on the snack cupboard! The best way for you to communicate with baby Aries is to make what you do and say as funny as possible. Aries has a great sense of humor, and will giggle for a long time when you make exaggerated gestures showing this little ram what could happen if she puts herself in harm's way by touching the stove or getting too close to the road. Before long, your little Aries will thank you for being as entertaining as you are loving and protective.

PISCES

Don't get scared when your Aries lets out loud screams and wails. There is little that's gentle or sensitive about your Aries child, but you will fall in love as you see how brave and noble she can be. Even as an infant, this child will seem like a hero. From the first time baby rolls over to the first walking steps, you'll be amazed at how—despite the danger of falling over or hitting that little head—your little one keeps trying, over and over, to get to the next stage.

The most important thing you can teach your Aries is to be more sensitive. It isn't a natural thing for Aries to care about how other people feel, and that would be opposite of the way you operate. Show Aries by example that by caring and sharing there is a lot to gain, including friendship, admiration, and love. Also, don't instill fear into this child. Despite your own sense of impending doom, you'll have to let go when Aries runs through the playground and climbs that ladder for the first time. You can't prevent every fall, but you can be close by enough to administer reassuring hugs (and Band-Aids).

CHAPTER 2

Taurus:

The Calm but Stubborn Bull

BORN BETWEEN: April 21–May 20
RULING PLANET: Venus – The earthy, sensorial side
EXALTED PLANET: The Moon
COLOR: Brown and Beige
GEMSTONES: Emerald and Peridot

*I*F YOU LOOK AT YOUR LITTLE ONE with the other Taurus infants in a hospital nursery, you may notice that they're not all thrashing and crying. Almost every Taurus is calm and gentle, and these traits come out in infancy more than they do at any other time. Conditions at the beginning of life are pretty much Taurus's idea of an ideal universe: There aren't any pressing matters to worry about, food and water come at regular intervals, people change your clothes for you, and wrap you in nice, snuggly blankets. Because your Taurus was born at the height of spring and has a *fixed* quality, can you blame this cute little darling for wanting to keep things exactly the way they are?

Taurus is always trying to protect the status quo. In some ways this can be good, because Taurus will go along with your plans for a regular daily schedule. Problems start when you disrupt this child's calm, gentle flow. The Taurus child takes to change only very slowly, and this can even result in their delaying taking steps toward growing up, particularly if those milestones involve taking on responsibility.

Taurus children are practical and productive, but not especially self-motivated. They are at their best when they are told exactly how something needs to be done and, under the right conditions, will be unusually compliant. There are, of course, some things Taurus won't like and when you have to persuade Taurus to do them anyway, you will be in for quite a battle! The quiet bundle of peace you just picked up from his nap can become stiff and stubborn enough at the mere suggestion of taking a bath to reveal why they call Taurus "The Bull." You have to bring Taurus along slowly, usually enticing this child with familiar toys and other appealing treats.

✳ YOUR TAURUS BOY ✳

Taurus boys are even-tempered and less likely to cause a big fuss in the sandbox than most other children. They'll play along with the others, and be especially kind to girls. This will make your Taurus boy very popular with the other parents as well as their children, and you'll be very proud you've given birth to such a balanced and calm child.

Then, one day, another child will try to take away one of baby Taurus's toys, or you or a caregiver might insist that he share what he has with another child. This, for the Taurus boy, is tantamount to an insult. Taurus boys do *not* like to give up what they have and will fight to keep hold of possessions with all their might. If you're lucky, your Taurus boy will be the kind who simply tries to outsmart everyone in order to avoid compliance with "share and share alike" mandates.

Taurus boys can be cutely conniving and clever, but they can also become physically aggressive. Other children who are silly enough to taunt Taurus or try to take something without his permission could get themselves hit, bitten, or kicked, leaving both you and your Taurus boy shocked at what he has just done! After all, his only intention was to protect what he has and save it from being ruined by someone who wasn't as conscientious about taking care of it.

Teach your Taurus boy the beauty of sharing and giving by example. Start him off at an early age by showing him how to share his toys and your attention with other children and people. You could even take him along while you volunteer at a home for ailing seniors and demonstrate how good it can feel to make someone smile. At home, get him involved in simple games that show him the value of waiting his turn and the fun he can have even when he doesn't win. This could be quite a trick, because your Taurus boy will like to bend the rules in such a way that he always, somehow, winds up being crowned King of the Hill or Mayor of Candy Land. He'll be happy every time it happens, too.

✳ YOUR TAURUS GIRL ✳

Taurus girls are steady and sweet, and for a while they'll play your games of dressing up like a miniature fairy princess. Your Taurus girl will love games that revolve around playing "house" and insist you look at her collection of teacups and dishes until you have an inventory of your own pictured in your mind. Enterprising and clever, your Taurus girl will have you thinking of what you can buy for her, even if you insist on leaving her with a sitter while you go out shopping for new clothes or shoes!

True to her acquisitive and protective nature, baby Taurus likes to *show* her toys, but sharing them is quite a different matter! You might want to have a talk with her before visitors arrive, and then allow her to take one (and only one) item that she wishes to protect and put it aside. This could stop her from throwing a major tantrum at the thought of others rifling through her precious possessions. When your little bull visits other households, though, she'll very much enjoy taking over the other child's privilege of ownership. Taurus girls might seem to be passive on the surface, but when they interact with their peers they can become quite domineering. Your daughter will want to make up the rules and dictate whose turn it is. Keep one ear on her to ensure she's not alienating herself from her friends' good graces.

Your Taurus girl will be well liked, but she likely won't want to have too many friends. She dislikes the disruption of playdates that include more than one other child, and she'll hope said playmate is at least as balanced and calm as she is. Give your Taurus girl the peace and quiet she needs, and don't worry about her preference for being with only one or two people at a time. She's not socially "backward," but she can be quite selective about who she spends time with! Usually, it will be someone she finds agreeable. At first she may show a preference for those she can easily dominate, but as she matures, she'll select friends who are as loyal, strong, and capable as she is!

✳ TALENTS AND AFFINITIES ✳

COLLECTING

Taurus gets a lot of satisfaction from acquiring items and keeping them where he or she can see them. Although Taurus can make occasional generous gestures, on the whole this child has a very strong sense of "mine," and gets comfort from having collections of things. This practice might start with stuffed animals or music boxes and progress later to more valuable items. Taurus is notorious for having expensive tastes, though, so start out with the age-appropriate and inexpensive.

LANGUAGE

Taurus takes in the world through the senses of touch and hearing, so language may come easily to your child. Books that allow tactile experiences as you introduce words will help the your little bull understand what talking is all about. As your baby learns new words, push him to use them when asking for food, drink, or a toy. If you don't, grunts, coos, and eventually, *screams*, will become your Taurus baby's way of getting what he wants.

BUILDING

Taurus is a constructive force, and that's why you'll notice your child's play preferences lean toward the purposeful sorts of activities. Shape sorters, building blocks and interlocking plastic pieces that form towers and cartoon figures will be favorites. Later in life, you might encourage this facility with model building or even video games that are geared toward creating cities, planets, and fantasy worlds of wonder.

✳ LITTLE CHALLENGES ✳

Taurus is such a calm and quiet baby, so why would you think twice about always providing whatever he seems to ask for? As baby Taurus grows, there will always be a part of your child that will want "more." That's why, at the outset, you must try to teach Taurus to be more self-sufficient and as ambitious as he is acquisitive. Of course, your baby won't want to have to bother to learn how to use the potty, tie shoes, or put on clothes without your loving assistance, but it's your job to teach technique and be strong enough to resist caving into Taurus's rather obstinate nature. You instantly adored everything about the quiet, placid bull Taurus embodies as an infant, but as this baby grows, you will see the threatening bovine with smoke coming out of its ears in your child, especially when Taurus isn't satisfied, doesn't want to do something, or is forced to share a favorite. You will have to understand this part of your child's personality, too. Taurus can very easily become one of those children who you hear demanding toys, food, and behavior from parents and caretakers as though he is the one in charge of the situation. If you want to avoid allowing your child to morph into a little dictator, you'll have to be strong, and just as stubborn as your little bull, especially in the throes of one of Taurus's infamous temper tantrums.

✳ DISCIPLINE ✳

Most of Taurus's slip-ups will have to do with refusing to do something you have asked, from picking up toys to brushing teeth or putting on shoes. Getting a Taurus to follow simple requests takes a lot of time. Always allow several extra minutes when you have to make it to an appointment or event on time, because prodding Taurus to make the transition from one kind of activity to the next isn't all that easy. This is especially true with video games and other activities that require follow-through. Because Taurus children are so good at finishing things they start, they become very upset when asked to stop when they're in the middle of something. The best way to get your child to interrupt "play" to get involved in "work" is to make steadfast rules. Set timers for the moment Taurus must get ready to leave the house or wash hands for dinner. It's harder to argue with a clock than a parent. Or, if you're truly desperate, take one or two items Taurus cherishes most, and keep them hidden away until your child displays the desired behavior. Next to his sense of security, possessions are the most important elements to Taurus's happiness.

FAVORITE THINGS

SING THESE SONGS WITH YOUR TAURUS CHILD

> **"Build a Home"**: For Taurus, this sounds like great fun.

> **"One More River to Cross"**: Ode to Noah's collection!

> **"Hush Little Baby"**: A billy goat *and* a diamond ring? Great!

WATCH MOVIES LIKE THIS WITH YOUR TAURUS CHILD

> *Toy Story:* To Taurus, possessions have personality.

> *Shrek:* Shows Taurus that sometimes it pays to wander out of the swamp.

> *Aladdin:* Every Taurus would love to make those wishes to a magical genie!

PLAY THESE GAMES WITH YOUR TAURUS CHILD

> **Camping Trip:** Exactly how much stuff would baby Taurus bring to the wilderness?

> **Red Light, Green Light:** Teaches Taurus the difference between stop and go!

> **Scavenger Hunt:** Could help Taurus learn how to get up and look for things.

READ THESE BOOKS, RHYMES, AND FAIRY TALES TO YOUR TAURUS CHILD

> *The Story of Ferdinand by Munro Leaf:* This story about a pacifist bull will allow Taurus to understand why we all like the placid one better.

> **"Come, Butter, Come":** Won't the cake just magically appear, after all?

> **"The Story of King Midas":** A little lesson about where extreme materialism might lead . . .

TREAT YOUR TAURUS CHILD TO THESE FOODS

> **Cheese:** Give Taurus a helping of texture, taste, and protein, in moderation.

> **Flavored Herbal Tea:** This will soothe Taurus's throat and fine-tune the palate.

> **Applesauce:** Smooth, delicious, and good for Taurus' comparatively slow-moving constitution.

Note: Taurus enjoys eating, and will be as much into the texture and temperature of the food as the taste. Definite tastes develop very early, so always present variety or you'll get one of those children who'll only eat white-colored foods like bread and cheese.

TAURUS'S BABY STYLE

Practical, but plush. Taurus likes clothes to be soft and comfortable. Your little bull won't choose bright colors, and is more content with quiet neutrals.

GIRLS: She'll be most comfy in crushed velvet or velour in winter; cool cotton in summer.

BOYS: Variety is far less important than ease of wear. The same shirt in various colors—or maybe only one or two—will be fine.

TAURUS'S ENVIRONMENT

Taurus will prefer to have one "quality" item as opposed to a room filled with various furnishings. A plush blanket will be especially comforting in the nursery, and a comfy stuffed chair might be a nice idea for baby's first piece of furniture.

CALMING TAURUS

Taurus children do cry sometimes, and usually it's because there is some sort of discomfort. Taurus doesn't ask for a lot of attention or demand entertainment; all you need to do is remain firm about delivering basic services on a regular schedule. This is one of the most difficult babies to deal with if you take a trip that involves time zones. Your little Taurus will take weeks to wake up on "vacation time," so jet lag will be a part of any vacation package deal. If you get overnight visitors, this too can disturb your little bull. She needs to go to bed and wake up as close to regular times as possible. When your Taurus is upset, calm voices and gentle rubs on the neck and around the ears will soothe hurt egos and make little bumps and bruises feel better. Your Taurus baby, despite the built-in stability and swagger, really needs you to deliver the reminder that everything will be all right.

STIMULATING TAURUS

Taurus will tend to do the same things over and over again, so you'll have to introduce new ideas and challenges for your child to try, such as:

- **Floor Puzzles:** Taurus will have to move around to put the pieces together.
- **Tactile Books:** Patting fake fur and little pieces of sandpaper create vivid images for Taurus.
- **Interlocking Bricks:** Always give Taurus opportunities to build things.

TAURUS'S LEARNING STYLE

Taurus learns by trial and error. If you see your child about to try to put a square peg into a round hole, let him experience how hard that is to do without saying a word. You might be surprised by how long your bull continues to try to do what he thought was right, and this isn't necessarily a bad trait. In school, you'll get reports about a very attentive and tenacious child who tackles challenges and stays with them to the finish.

PARENTING TAURUS

If your sign is . . .

ARIES

This quiet, peaceful little baby surely does seem innocent enough. What more can you ask for than an infant who allows you to go on with your life while sleeping unobtrusively, whether swaddled and tucked away in the nursery, wrapped up to run around on four wheels, or slung on your body in a safe-but-cozy carrier? Indeed, the Taurus child's placidity is a great virtue, but you'd be mistaken if you were to believe it was always going to be this easy to get the baby to go along with your wishes.

There are basic differences between you and Taurus that you're going to have to resolve. Chief among them is the fact you're always on the go, and Taurus would far prefer to remain undisturbed. Strapping baby Taurus into a jogger stroller, for instance, might not be such a good idea; and once that stubborn streak starts to develop, it might turn out to be impossible. Taurus's will is just as strong as yours, so you'll both have to meet in the middle. If you slow down, and feed Taurus activities in small bites, you'll both enjoy the journey toward growing up.

TAURUS

You can't complain about having a baby who doesn't make a lot of noise, and—just like you—enjoys peace, quiet, and regular routine. From the time you meet your child, you'll be enamored with the way he seems to go right along with your suggestions. The honeymoon period of early infancy will allow you to bond well enough to discover how deeply you love this child, but it will be over too soon. Once your Taurus is autonomous enough to resist you, a battle of sorts will be on.

Raising this child will require you to confront your own inflexibility so you can show your bull how to become less immovable. This doesn't mean you should give in to your child's whims; but it will mean you can show how "nice" it is to compromise by example. The art of negotiation is innate to the Taurus character, even if the starting position is usually some form of "It's *all* mine . . . ." Play games that teach your child how important it is to know that you can't have everything you want—and you'll both learn some valuable lessons along the way.

GEMINI

You'll marvel at the contentment you see behind every smile your Taurus gives you. This quiet infant is a pleasure to have in your household. You'll be relieved that you don't have to spend most nights up trying to devise ways of making a crying baby realize that it's time to sleep. You'll also enjoy watching your child apply each thing he learns to practical skills, and you'll be proud of the way your Taurus achieves different levels of development right on schedule, if not sooner.

You and your little bull have very different ways of communicating, though. You like to verbalize your thoughts, while Taurus takes sensations and feelings and expresses them on a subtler level, usually by appearing agitated. If your Taurus is upset, it's usually because you forgot to do something that you always do, such as turn on the musical lamp before a nap. Use your wit and your patience to weather occasional tantrums, but never give in; Taurus needs to curb some of those domineering traits. This bull needs consistent routine, and you tend to opt for constant variety, so you'll have to work to teach one another that there's no one "right" way to see the world, or to share a lifetime.

CANCER

Your Taurus child will be exceptionally receptive to your attentive and nurturing parenting skills, and you'll like the way your little bull drinks in all the love you have to give. There's something about the look on your child's face that says "Thank you for caring for me," and you might also sense that she picks up your feelings, too. This might be true to some degree, but don't expect Taurus to be as sensitive and sympathetic as you are. Taurus can be kind, but isn't overly generous or understanding.

In fact, you'll have to avoid appearing to be a pushover. When your child gets a bit bossy, as Taurus will, you must show that your kind and gentle manner doesn't prevent you from standing up for yourself. You can respond to your child's need for consistent routine without agreeing to get stuck into an inalterable rut. Be firm and unyielding when it comes to standing up to a Taurus temper tantrum. The two of you can be very good friends, but this will work for you only as long as you retain your role as parent, provider, and—much to the chagrin of your Taurus child—"boss."

LEO

Your Taurus child will make you proud from the outset because there is a calm dignity about this baby that isn't too much different than your own. While not showy or dramatic, Taurus babies are extremely forceful. You'll find out more about this when and if you "lock horns" over issues such as when Taurus is going to take a nap or go to the doctor's office and get there on time.

Your sense of leadership as discipline is excellent for the Taurus. You have high expectations, and Taurus will feel almost dared to reach them. Although Taurus may not seem competitive, your child will be very eager to show you that she is a force to be reckoned with. In fact, once the baby passes through the first several weeks of life, Taurus becomes very willful and stubborn; it won't be all that easy to convince this child to do things your way, but as a parent, that's what you must do. Obviously, you'll have to stand up to this child at a much earlier age than you might guess, and it's important not to be *too* harsh. Taurus will eventually learn who's boss, and you'll do a convincing job of identifying that person to be you.

VIRGO

It might feel like your Taurus is your "little friend" from a very early time in his life. Peaceful and practical, cuddly and orderly, this baby seems to be customized to make your life complete. There are, indeed, many traits that you and your Taurus baby share: You're both practical, thrive in a peaceful environment, and enjoy nature. But there are some differences too, though, and you'll need to be aware of them.

Although you're widely known for making meticulously detailed plans, you can change them if situations dictate that you must. Taurus is not as flexible as you are. Your child will try to remove obstacles, including other people's needs and demands, so things can be done in his own way. This could be a cause of friction between you, to say the least, and standing your ground in a dispute with this persevering little person will be a challenge. You must stick to your rules, though, and avoid allowing Taurus to perceive a "win," or else every time you need to distract Taurus from what he or she is doing, you're going to have to go through a "battle royale" that you'd certainly rather avoid.

LIBRA

You and your Taurus baby will be very happy to meet one another. You share a peaceful attitude and both enjoy the finer things in life. Your little Taurus won't be noisy or fussy, especially not at first. The calm manner of this placid sign will dominate, until Taurus comes to realize, usually during the first several months of life, that you will not always want to deliver exactly what this little bull wants.

All children have moments when they fight their parents for the privilege of doing whatever they wish. Taurus does this more tenaciously than most, and will prolong a battle especially because the fighting itself seems to upset you. Because you're a parent now, you can't just walk away from the argument. When pressed to a certain point, you'll probably deploy your skills in diplomacy and use them to regain peace in your household. As long as you don't negotiate your authority away, this might work out. You'll learn to be a fair and reliable authority figure, and you might also teach baby Taurus that there's such a thing as "give and take," and when we give, it can be even better than getting!

SCORPIO

Your little Taurus will hold a strong—and strange—attraction for you. Although the two of you know how different you are in many ways, there is a certain commonality that will make you perfect learning partners in this parent-child relationship. The Taurus baby will be quiet and peaceful for the most part, and won't complain as long as you provide the basics.

When the child grows, and you begin to try to impose your will upon your little Taurus, you will meet with a will that's as strong as yours—well, almost, anyway. Both you and your baby want to be the dominant person in this relationship, and because you're the parent, you must ensure that that person is you. This has to happen if you want the rest of the world to see your child in the same light that you do. You won't have problems doing this, but it will be a constant struggle. You might not be used to having people question your authority this way, but having this little person push your buttons can teach you about staying strong, while becoming at least a tiny bit flexible.

SAGITTARIUS

Your precious Taurus, un-fussed by most of what goes on around her, brings you a lot of joy. You will be grateful for this child's easygoing attitude as you fumble your way through changing your first diapers. As long as Taurus is taken care of, there isn't much this little one finds to be ticked off about. What you might not find out until baby Taurus is a bit older is just how little what you say will determine what she does. This baby is not a pushover, and will let you know it through some rather strong outbursts.

When this happens, you might want to throw up your hands and run for professional help, but that's not really necessary. As the parent, you have to take Taurus's considerable energy and contain it so it can be used for practical purposes. Teach little Taurus to be more malleable by rewarding your baby with goofy voices and gags. Your child's sense of humor will certainly grow strong, after being guided by a parent who's as fun as you are, while being a great teacher, too.

CAPRICORN

You and your Taurus will have an easy time getting used to one another. You're both focused on pretty much the same things. You like comfort and want to do useful things in the world. Comparatively calm for a child, Taurus desires comfort and may not be all that interested in the getting down to work part. You must provide the things you are so good at demonstrating—motivation and dedication.

Your little bull has a tendency to maintain the status quo, so you must point out what happens when we try harder. Broaden Taurus's perspective by playing with building toys together or with trips to a local attraction that let Taurus get hands-on experiences that reveal the challenges of science, music, and the arts. This child should not be over-stimulated, but you'll know just how much new material is needed as Taurus reaches little plateaus. Although you'll be tempted to shower your child with educational toys and gifts, the very best present you can give to Taurus is your time. Carve out a piece of every day so both of you can enjoy your relationship.

AQUARIUS

The Taurus child is definitely a gift from the heavens, and you appreciate her tenacity and determination a much as you thank her for not constantly crying and fussing. Taurus has a certain quality that makes you sure that, with your help, your little bull is on her way to becoming one of the world's most outstanding citizens.

You'll want to instill certain values into your Taurus child, but you must understand what matters most in her little mind. Security, in the very down-to-earth and material sense, will be the thing that motivates your child. You can make sure most of these physical needs are provided, but you also must encourage baby Taurus to work on her own self-sufficiency in age-appropriate and educational ways. Avoid relegating your parenting duties to gadgets such as video games and so-called "interactive" toys. Your child really needs to have a deep connection with you if you expect to pass on your values, and you need to teach Taurus that while it's good to take care of oneself, we must also contribute to the wider community. Your creative take on the world will baffle Taurus at times, but you'll use it to create a unique experience that will make growing up fun for your Taurus baby.

PISCES

The cute and cuddly Taurus child will make your heart swell with love! You'll enjoy taking care of his basic needs for food, shelter, and cleanliness because he will seem to be so grateful. This will be the case, for sure, if you do all of this consistently. Taurus is a creature of habit, and because you most certainly are not, you'll have to work extra hard at keeping a regular schedule.

Your little Taurus can be sweet and kind, but he is rarely anywhere near as generous as you. In fact, you'll find yourself encouraging this tyke to share toys and not take all the goodies on a regular basis. Taurus's acquisitive nature isn't mean-spirited in the least. This little child merely wants to conserve resources and protect them from being squandered. Still, you have to teach Taurus how to trust others, and that sharing goes in both directions. If anyone can, you can bring Taurus to the realization that getting and having is nice, but sharing is even better. Use your imagination to tell stories and get Taurus involved in activities that teach these lessons early on. That way, the only calls you get from teachers will be notifications of awards and scholarships!

CHAPTER 3

Gemini:

Watch Baby Work the Room

BORN BETWEEN: May 21–June 20
RULING PLANET: Mercury – the daytime, chatty and quick-thinking trickster side
EXALTED PLANET: Mercury
COLOR: Steel Blue, Silver
GEMSTONES: Aquamarine, Euclase

THAT PLEASANT AND ACTIVE BUNDLE you're cuddling is one of the most social babies you'll ever meet, so enjoy holding your baby Gemini in your arms while you can. Once he can get up and run around, you won't see nearly as much of each other! Gemini is an *air* sign, and born during the time spring turns to summer, making this child a *mutable* personality. Your child will grow up with little question about the purpose of every Gemini's life: to find out what's going on and report it as much and to as many people as possible. Most Gemini babies have a very active dialogue going on in their minds, so don't assume that your child is merely an infant with little or no cognitive capacity.

Geminis will begin to communicate almost immediately, even if they can't talk or move around much in their swaddling blankets. They'll use their eyes to tell you they want to connect, and stare at you while you feed them. Gemini's also try to talk as soon as possible. Even if it's just quiet cooing, your newborn will vocalize, often just to test out the basic speaking apparatus! Lips, tongue, and vocal chords are precious equipment to your baby, and there will be much fascination with them. The arms, hands, and fingers are also points of focus on Gemini's body, so you'll notice your baby playing with them more than other infants do. Gemini babies also look around a lot. They like to take in everything, and strive to engage everyone in the room at the same time. Your Gemini takes in the world through sound and sight more than touch, but that doesn't mean you should omit the usual amount of holding or rocking. All children, even your self-reliant and irrepressible Gemini, need to gain some sense of security from parent-to-child bodily contact.

✳ YOUR GEMINI BOY ✳

Gemini boys might not seem as "rough and tumble" as you would expect a male child to be and they're typically not all that interested in fighting or being overly aggressive. Like all people born under signs that manifest the element of air, Gemini wants to be liked and appreciated by others. This explains part of the reason why he may seem passive, at least physically. In his mind, your Gemini boy could be waging a wild battle as he watches other children fighting, pulling for the one he hopes will win. He's far too busy taking mental notes to participate in the fray; he has to get every detail down pat so he can tell the rest of the gang about the event.

Your Gemini boy will have to learn how to defend himself, certainly, but for the most part he isn't the kind of person a bully will pick on. Besides, your Gemini boy has probably also found a way to befriend the bully! These charming souls, filled with personality, make connections with everyone. Sometimes there's little or no "like" involved. Gemini boys often size up how a person can help them and then decide it would be a good idea to become good buddies, or at least playground pals.

Speaking of companionship, your Gemini boy needs a lot of it. He won't be able to be around children all of the time, so he'll rely on you to be his sounding board. In the preverbal stages, your Gemini baby will try to engage you in some favorite games and will always love it when you read or tell him a story.

Give your Gemini boy lots of information and attention. The more time you can spend talking to him, even before he has really decoded language, the better; your Gemini boy will understand, on his level, that you're a reliable source of information. Later, when big questions arise, he'll know it's safe to come to you and you'll begin to build what is sure to become a fun and fantastic friendship.

✳ YOUR GEMINI GIRL ✳

Your jabbering baby doll is sure to provide plenty of entertainment! She'll be very sweet to you, and very curious about the world surrounding her. Always give her plenty of mental stimulation because she takes in the world through sight and sound, for the most part. You may have to work extra hard to teach her about touching things that are dangerous or venturing to places that don't even resemble solid ground.

Because all Gemini girls will want to know what's going on beyond the walls of the nursery, you might have to childproof your home with more attentiveness than you might have expected when you first learned your child was female. You might not think a girl would be as prone to roam as your little Gemini, but she may develop locomotion skills more quickly than other female babies, due to her drive to get up, out, and about. Although they're not necessarily natural-born athletes, Gemini girls do tend to move around a lot and will wander off if you're not watching their every move.

Keep your Gemini girl engaged with an interesting environment and amusing toys. When she is bored, she can become impatient. Avoid placating her exclusively with passive activities such as audio and video entertainment designed for babies and children, though. When she fusses, consider instead a ride in the car or a walk that allows her to watch the world go by from the comfort of her stroller. She likes to interact rather than be merely entertained, and she'll particularly enjoy sharing the experience with you. Teach her that it's a good thing to reach out to socialize to other people. She's going to tend to do this anyway, but with your encouragement she'll build extra self-esteem and confidence.

Gemini girls like to have a lot of friends, and they will go to great lengths to win them and to keep them. It's really important to ensure that your Gemini girl knows she's fabulous, whether she's just like everyone else or not. Otherwise, she could be susceptible to "copycat" behavior. She'll want what all the other girls have just so she can get them to relate to her. Although there's little harm in her wanting the same barrette set or headband her friends have at twelve months, at twelve years this issue can become far more damaging. Your Gemini girl may seem to be very independent and uninterested in you at times, but in truth she's watching your every move. Make sure she knows you're there for her, 100 percent.

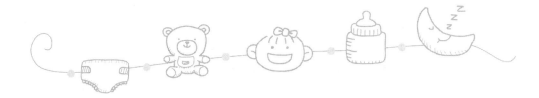

✳ TALENTS AND AFFINITIES ✳

MANUAL DEXTERITY

Gemini has an unusual ability to use her hands to manipulate the objects she finds around the nursery and the rest of the house. No electrical outlet or stove knob can be assumed to be safe from a Gemini child on the move! On the bright side, this baby holds toys and grabs for food far ahead of schedule, and will rely less on you for simple tasks such as these.

LANGUAGE

Some Gemini children start to try to talk right away, while others take their time. Still, one thing remains consistent across the board: Once they start talking, they don't stop! Your little Gemini will be relentless at questioning the names for common objects and will put words together almost magically. You might be tired by the end of the day, but before long you'll discover how much fun it is to take care of a baby who communicates so well.

PLAYFULNESS

Gemini loves to play! Your little one will make a game out of just about anything, from eating to putting away the toys for the day. This makes it easy to manage your Gemini child, at least through the first months and years. You'll have to keep up with your child's games if you want to stay in them, though! This means you might have to relearn checkers or chess, or master the art of video gaming.

FAVORITE THINGS

SING THESE SONGS WITH YOUR GEMINI CHILD

> **"ABC song":** For Gemini, no such thing as learning it too early.

> **"Head, Shoulders, Knees and Toes":** Mini-tour of Gemini's body via the hands.

> **"Farmer in the Dell":** This one covers a lot of gossip in a few verses.

WATCH MOVIES LIKE THIS WITH YOUR GEMINI CHILD

> *Alice in Wonderland:* The adventures inside the rabbit hole will be riveting.

> *The Muppet Movie:* Nothing like singing, laughing characters on a cross-country trip to inspire Gemini's roaming spirit.

> *Winnie The Pooh:* Gemini will adore meeting all the characters and admiring their personalities and interactions.

PLAY THESE GAMES WITH YOUR GEMINI CHILD

> **Chess:** No kidding. Gemini can handle it sooner than you think.

> **Hand Clap Games:** Tricks Gemini into thinking he's found a twin!

> **Telephone:** Of course Gemini will want to test how well the message is passed!

READ THESE BOOKS, RHYMES, AND FAIRY TALES TO YOUR GEMINI CHILD

> *The Tale of Peter Rabbit by Beatrix Potter:* A tale of mischief, misbehavior, and forgiveness.

> **"Wee Willie Winkie":** Gemini will love this tale of Willie running all around the town.

> **"The Turtle and the Swans":** Even flying turtles have to keep their mouths shut sometimes!

TREAT YOUR GEMINI CHILD TO THESE FOODS

> **Finger Food:** Your little Gemini loves to eat on the go, so he will gobble up little crackers and string cheese.

> **Apple Juice:** Clear, sweet, and soothing on the vocal chords.

> **Cherries:** They're quick to eat and require deft hands.

LITTLE CHALLENGES

Geminis can be hard to hold, in more than one way; these children are not excessively dependent on home and family, and they typically resent it when you try to hold them back in any way. Gemini's ideal world is one where he is permitted to interact with anyone and everyone, at any time. Your biggest problems will probably start with enforcing naptime and bedtime.

For your mental health a well as for the sake of your little Gemini's normal and functional development, rest is a necessity, not an option. Set times for these rest periods and stick to them. Institute routines that include a lot of interaction and two-way communication prior to the lights going out. If your Gemini refuses to accept the end of this time and the beginning of the isolation required for proper rest, don't negotiate. Be sweet, be kind, and be gentle, but be firm.

Gemini children also have a tendency to avoid telling the truth when it might incriminate themselves or others. Gemini doesn't really mean to lie, but when it's convenient, your child will find a way to believe both what is real and what he has invented as the most expedient way to avoid punishment.

DISCIPLINE

The Gemini child's primary directive, remember, is to be free to learn and spread news about other people. When you prevent this, especially by isolating her, you will provoke your child into making elaborate plans to escape and remain free to roam! In infancy, this may consist of kicking and screaming; but as your Gemini child grows older, more intricate webs will be woven.

The idea of being "grounded" might sound more appropriate for an adolescent child's punishment, but in Gemini's case it's a good concept to introduce; feel free to use "grounding" as a way of expressing your disapproval. If Gemini doesn't stop talking in a setting that demands quiet, such as a church, a theater, or an important civil ceremony, removing her from the opportunity to interact with people, both during and after the event, clearly states the behavior was undesirable. Then, when you remove Gemini's privileges to meet and greet because she was untruthful to you, the message will be rather clear.

GEMINI'S BABY STYLE

Sleek, with a streak of trendiness. Gemini likes to be on top of the latest fads and will feel out of place if not dressed somewhat like her peers. You don't have to cave to this faddishness, but within reason, you need to respond to your Gemini child's need to fit in.

GIRLS: Your Gemini girl is going to want to wear pretty clothes that feature popular cartoon characters, but will gleefully dress up in a cute skirt with matching top and shoes, especially if they're in tones of light blue or silvery gray.

BOYS: Gemini boys don't want to wear things that make them stand out from the crowd. Stick with plain-colored shirts and blue jeans on the bottom. Baby clothes should be comfortable enough to allow Gemini to move freely.

GEMINI ENVIRONMENT

Use pastel colors and accents of futuristic metallic and fluorescent tones in Gemini's nursery. These hues feel like "home" and will create a space your baby enjoys inhabiting. This little arrangement also increases your chances of getting your Gemini to stay in the room when appropriate.

✳ CALMING GEMINI ✳

Gemini can be nervous, so when there is a lot of crying, remain calm. Rather than becoming frustrated with your Gemini, simply create a more peaceful and less distracting space by limiting noise. Remove sources of stimulation, ranging from a group of playmates to a loud TV. Hold your child just tightly enough to let her know that she is safe, but don't grab on too tightly. Relaxation for Gemini will always equate with some elements of freedom as well as security.

✳ STIMULATING GEMINI ✳

Your Gemini child is intelligent, to be sure, but if you want your baby to also be "smart" you'll have to develop Gemini's capacity to maintain an attention span. Try some of these toys and tools:

- **Shape Sorter:** Make a game out of getting them all "right."
- **Puppets:** Help Gemini act out those evil acts of his "evil twin."
- **Puzzles:** Don't let Gemini give up. Offer rewards (a trip to the zoo?) for finishing it.

✳ GEMINI'S LEARNING STYLE ✳

Gemini takes in information by listening and this is where the problems begin. Most Gemini children don't stop talking long enough to listen, which is why it's so important to teach them the art and the beauty of silence. Take your Gemini out in nature to notice how quiet it is, and point out how much she can learn without words. As long as they are taught to focus, Gemini children pick up the rest without a problem.

PARENTING GEMINI

If your sign is . . .

ARIES

You might be amazed to find out how quickly your little Gemini comes to understand everything you say. That's why it's especially important to avoid using words you wouldn't want your child to repeat! Gemini also will be very sensitive to your temper and mood. Although this child seems to be detached from emotions, Gemini can become very nervous. You'll know you're being too rough for your baby when she cries without any obvious reason, moves those little hands around randomly, and maybe even starts to quiver.

The very best way to calm your Gemini baby down is to talk directly to your child and use a calm and soothing tone of voice. You may have only been upset because your team made a stupid play; but your Gemini baby might have thought all that yelling and screaming was due to some kind of unwanted baby behavior. Your Gemini child will love your sense of humor, so feel free to be as "goofy" as you like. This child will also be fond of adventure, and you may spend many summer vacations exploring and investigating new places together.

TAURUS

You might have some trouble figuring out what you're supposed to do with your Gemini child. While you're utterly content to sit still and barely look up from whatever is amusing you, your Gemini's curiosity will send him off on minute-by-minute adventures. This child is all about constant chatter and motion, but if you think you can get Gemini to give up on the act of constant surveillance, forget it.

You're going to have to compromise with your child by going out more often than you want to, and you'll also need to teach your Gemini to be content with staying still, at least for part of the day. You could, for example, take him out to a playground or even for rides in the car. Let your Gemini do the socializing! Yours is the child who smiles and waves and wants to see everyone. Thank goodness it's only a superficial kind of thing. Baby Gemini rarely gets so entranced that you can't move on, get back in the car, and go toward that nice peaceful day at home you were hoping for from the beginning.

GEMINI

Having this baby born under the same sign as you is like a dream come true. The two of you can have fascinating conversations from the get-go. No matter if all you say is "ga-ga, goo-goo," the two of you will enjoy connecting, sharing knowing looks, and bonding as the best buddies you are. It's going to be hard for you to remember that you're supposed to be the authority figure in this relationship, so you'll have to be careful about keeping your distance and retaining your role as disciplinarian.

This will mean you also have to allow your little one to be a child. It will be very tempting to treat your Gemini as an equal, but it's your job to ensure that she knows how to behave within the reasonable boundaries of the rest of the world. Just like you, this child has problems keeping quiet, and will often speak out of turn at school and at inappropriate times. Play games that prove that listening is just as crucial as speaking, and your Gemini child will learn this lesson and have fun doing it.

CANCER

Don't worry so much about your Gemini. It's very normal for this little bundle of energy to move around a lot, kick off blankets, and look from one side to another nervously. Because of the child's tendency to be high-strung, you have to avoid picking up on this energy and be even calmer than you might already feel. Rather than cradling the baby and trying to make little Gemini stay still, focus on finding what makes him feel good and doing that. Most of the time, Gemini will respond to your voice. When you can't focus your attention on talking or reading a story, play nice, lively music for your Gemini.

Gemini is a bit of a trickster, so your tendency to think the best of everyone—especially your child—is going to leave lots of leeway. If all little Gemini does is steal one of your lovingly baked homemade cookies, you won't care; but you need to teach your child that taking things without permission isn't something people should do. Also, don't let Gemini's aloof attitude hurt your feelings. This baby isn't nearly as overtly loving—or loyal—as you are. Still, later in life, the two of you will enjoy the bond you develop, even if it isn't as emotionally based as you may wish.

LEO

Your little Gemini will respond well to your strong leadership and bold parenting style, as long as you're wise enough to leave her some extra space. You understand one another very well, and eventually Gemini will respect you without being afraid of you or cynical about your methods. During infancy, though, you'll have to establish a strong foundation by mixing your authoritative manner with gentleness. When Gemini fusses, it might be because there haven't been enough trips around the block. Always try to take Gemini along with you. Going to the grocery store is an adventure for this social little baby, and you'll all enjoy it much more when you go as a family.

You are usually pretty firm about your rules, and you can plan on your Gemini trying to outwit you in order to find ways around them. This baby loves mischief, and when he misbehaves, it is his way of really asking you to figure out what's going on and stop the deviant behavior. You're sharp enough to see what's coming before your Gemini even thinks it through, which makes you and your Gemini an almost-perfect parent-child match.

VIRGO

You'll relate to your little Gemini on a very basic level because you both share the desire to collect and sort through information. You'll watch your baby looking around the room with wonder and share in the excitement of every new discovery.

Where you and your Gemini child might differ, though, will be in what you do with the information once you get it. Far more capable of discerning what's worth knowing and what's just "garbage," you'll wonder indeed why your Gemini child is always talking about the minutiae of other people's comings and goings.

This won't stop Gemini from giving you all the news there is to know anyway! Your need for peace and quiet might mean you get up an hour or so before Gemini's normal rising time. Even as an infant, your Gemini will be demanding of your attention, and when he gets older, he'll insist you teach the fine points of object naming and vocalizing. Try not to be dismissive, and never assume Gemini is "too young" to be read to or included in conversations. Use your awesome teaching skills to help with Gemini's development, and you'll be rewarded with a child whose rich communication talents will always be a source of pride.

LIBRA

You and your little Gemini will get along really well. This child doesn't require constant soothing or coddling, and will react positively to the peaceful surroundings you create. The only thing that could make it somewhat different might be the endless chatter that your child engages in. From birth, the Gemini baby obviously loves the sound of her own voice. Don't worry! This doesn't mean there will be a lot of crying, but it does mean that little Gemini will constantly compete for your attention, and will insist you not only listen, but also respond, to random utterances as well as nonverbal cues.

Gemini respects your intellect, and like you, needs to have someone around at all times. "Is this right?" will be the question Gemini conveys with a querulous look the first time she picks up a toy, and will insist that you respond. This won't go on forever, so you might want to take these opportunities to offer your opinions, and most important, set your boundaries. Your distaste for conflict could lead you to let Gemini "just go," but you'll live to regret this course if you pursue it. Always let Gemini know there's zero chance of her outwitting a smart parent like you.

SCORPIO

Like two people sitting back-to-back, you and your little Gemini will love being together but you'll have two wholly different perspectives on the world. While you like to take deliberate action, working on one thing at a time, your baby will be the ultimate multitasker. Even during infancy, Gemini will want more visual and tactile stimulation than you might think a baby can handle. Later, once she begins to crawl around, you'll be somewhat overwhelmed by the task of keeping up. Yet, before long, you'll figure out more than one way to keep Gemini safely contained. The basic difference between the two of you is the way you need to go way in to depth in order to understand what's going on around you. Gemini, on the other hand, finds it easiest to dabble only on the superficial level, covering as much territory as possible.

You might want to teach Gemini to balance that urge to scatter attention and effort by demonstrating the benefits of that one little word, "focus." You can't change Gemini's disposition or tendencies, but you can make her think about the utility of paying attention to one thing at a time, especially as she gets to be of school age. Use your wisdom—and thoughtful discipline.

SAGITTARIUS

How exciting! A little Gemini you can talk to and run around after, and later, go on adventures with! You'll certainly relate to Gemini's desire to remain untethered, but to some degree you'll both have to work on keeping one another grounded. Funny enough, when you focus on the needs of your child to assimilate and blend in with the rest of humanity, this will happen pretty much on its own. The worst thing you can do for your Gemini child is treat him like your new best friend. Always remember that the two of you were brought together for a special purpose—but you're the teacher, and your baby is the student.

The topic of learning is a good one to keep Gemini aware of at all times. This child's natural curiosity will lead to many questions, a fascination with games, and a tendency to go from one thing to the next, which may make learning in school a challenge. Give your Gemini a good start by avoiding overstimulation, especially when Gemini is learning words, ABCs, or numbers. If you take the time to enjoy teaching, and make it fun but focused, both you and your Gemini will cherish knowledge even more.

CAPRICORN

Your Gemini, an information-gathering machine, will baffle you when you first get to know him. This little one is far more verbal (and verbose) than you'll ever be, and even before words begin to form, you'll notice your child struggling to understand what is supposed to be said and how to say it. Being amused rather than annoyed is a good idea, because you won't be able to change this essential Gemini trait. All you'll be able to accomplish is some moments of quiet now and then, mostly while baby Gemini is asleep.

Your baby won't cry all that much; in fact, Gemini is a good sport and takes most things in stride. When he does get upset, check for hunger, a dirty diaper, sleepiness, or the most likely cause—boredom. Gemini is very intelligent, and thrives on stimulation. You might want to get one of those "busybox" toys and place it in the crib long before you expected that you'd have to. Use electronic toys with care, though. Gemini is so enamored by anything that's techie-friendly that your baby could lose an entire childhood within the eerie blue glow of a video screen.

AQUARIUS

You'll see right away how wonderful it is that you've been sent this adorable Gemini child to love. You will be able to pick up on one another's thoughts and feelings, and you'll adore watching your little one collect information and use it to keep tabs on everyone he meets. As time goes on, you'll thrive on using your parental skills to help Gemini learn new vocabulary, even nonverbal gestures that predate actual talking. Your child's sharp mind will amaze you, yet you may grow frustrated when Gemini sometimes squanders intellect in exchange for being charming and popular.

It's important to remember that children are given to parents for the purpose of a mutual learning experience. Could it be that you need to focus on the small stuff far more often than you do? Ask that question when you notice your Gemini working the room at the playgroup or while he's giving you the rundown on each and every one of the other kids in the sandbox. You'll come to admire Gemini's people skills, and view them as a tool that will serve your child in years to come. You'll also discover how love isn't always all about making people behave the way you want them to!

PISCES

You and your little Gemini share a bond that won't be obvious at first. Although you're quieter and less outgoing than this child, the both of you have a very deep interest in other people. The difference is that you pick up on feelings, while Gemini picks up on thoughts, opinions, and "back-stories." Of course, you may not be able to jointly conquer a networking event while Gemini is still cooing in your arms, but understanding this about your child will help you to relate even better to each other. It will be fun to watch how your child tries to make people smile and you'll be in awe of how easy this is for Gemini to do.

Raising a Gemini will also be challenging, because you'll have to struggle to create appropriate rules and limitations. Cultivating respect from this child will depend on your ability to read through her charming wit and sheepish grins. You'll have to point out to Gemini when it's time to place more concern on others and not merely study them on the superficial level. Make eye contact with this child from the moment you see one another, and your Gemini will realize that universal love is all that really matters.

CHAPTER 4

Cancer:

The Natural Nurturer

BORN BETWEEN: June 21–July 21
RULING PLANET: Moon – Changeable and elusive
EXALTED PLANET: Jupiter
COLOR: Sea Green
GEMSTONES: Ruby, Moonstone

HE SWEET, QUIET, AND SENSITIVE CANCER CHILD seems to be vulnerable, but don't be fooled. This little one came into the world at the beginning of summer, so there's a certain persistence about Cancer's temperament that mirrors the strength of the sun at its most potent time of the year. Cancer is very much a self-starting *cardinal* sign, but it is also a *water* sign, so your child's emotions will waver and flow, just like the ocean! Yes, this sounds sweet, but oftentimes it will seem as though Cancer's feelings come on more like the onrush of a pelting rain—sometimes, a tsunami. This baby will cry for no apparent reason, and as you make further attempts to avoid the outbursts you may come to feel as though you're walking on eggshells.

Cancer needs more than the normal amount of soothing and reassurance. To some degree, you can address this with coddling and protection, but be careful. You will want to balance all that extra TLC with an equal amount of teaching about how to survive in a world that will not always be entirely hospitable. Be understanding, but firm, during times when baby Cancer must learn the art of survival. This child, though potentially a strong, capable, and fierce nurturer, starts out life just *loving* to be a baby. Throughout life, your child will go back and forth between the polar opposites of taking care of others and wanting to be taken care of. It's your job, as the parent, to show your little crab that life will consist of experiences on both ends of the spectrum and lots of other moments that fall in between. Teach Cancer that it's all right to cry, but only when there's a viable reason.

YOUR CANCER BOY

The Cancer boy will be quieter than most, but if you encourage the right traits he can become strong and reliable, too. Because the act of nurturing, Cancer's main characteristic, is often assumed to be a female trait, you might not see the worth of fostering it in your Cancer boy; but in fact, the best thing you can do for him is teach him how to take care of others. Start small with a stuffed toy or an established family pet and show him that this entity needs his attention and care. Drawing his attention outward will help to ameliorate the overly emotional and self-centered features of his personality. You won't want your Cancer child to grow into a man who wants to remain an infant for his whole life. It's very tempting to coddle him and give into his emotional storms, but if you do, he has much to lose.

The Cancer boy probably won't have an innate affinity for activities such as contact sports or car racing. These activities make more noise than he probably wants to hear. He'll do well at other male-oriented activities such as building and home repair, though. Equip him with a plastic tool set at an early age, and watch him go to "work." As he grows, he might develop an interest in road construction and home building that goes a little deeper than the average. He'll also display talents for music, art, and cooking. Instead of dismissing his gentler side, it's far wiser to give him opportunities to express his emotions through safe channels such as the arts, and to learn about the care of others through cooking and tending to pets. In school, the Cancer boy might not be the first to shout out answers or raise his hand to volunteer. That's why you must empower him with the gift of being the authority over a building process, a work of art, or an animal.

YOUR CANCER GIRL

Depending on the family dynamics, your Cancer girl can start out life soft and tender or valiant and strong; much depends on what you expect of her and how hard she must vie for your attention. However, in the end, she'll be a bit of each. If there is competition from siblings, she could use either extreme passivity or a more aggressive approach to stake her claim on her place in the family pecking order. If she is an only child, you would do well to place some kind of competition in her way to help her build the strong part of her character. This doesn't mean you should ignore her or push her away, but if you denote clear boundaries around being interrupted during things like telephone conversations and while working around the home, your Cancer girl will learn it's okay for her to have boundaries, too.

This is a crucial lesson for her to learn, because her sensitivity leads her to literally pick up on the moods of those around her and mirror them in her effort to be loved by them. If you leave her un-empowered, your Cancer girl could fall prey to peer pressure much more easily than you would like.

You can push her toward independent thinking by encouraging her to take up activities that allow her to show her "power." This could include martial arts, gymnastics, and music lessons. Provide her with a variety of toys, but always include baby dolls and stuffed animals among them. Cancer is, more than anything, a nurturer, and your little girl will take great pleasure in playing "Mommy." Watch her closely for clues—as she acts out the roles and talks about her dollies' families, you'll discover the things she's picking up from you.

Cancer girls are like super-absorbent sponges, and they do take in and retain far more than we wish they would. Your little girl will remember most of the details of her childhood based on the sensations, experiences, and emotions she has during her formative years. Make sure first and foremost among them is the sensation of being protected and loved!

✷ TALENTS AND AFFINITIES ✷

COOKING AND PARENTING

Cancer likes to make a nest wherever she goes; you might notice this by taking a quick look in her crib. Most likely, an entire collection of stuffed animals, plus a few favorite articles of clothing (and maybe a "blankie") will be in there most of the time. Be aware that Cancer's fascination for survival drives this child to a more intense curiosity about cooking than you might guess. Protect your little Cancer from obvious dangers, but do let her in on food preparation duties when you can. Cooking is a great life skill!

LANGUAGE

The one complaint that most people have about Cancer children is their tendency to whine. The wail you hear coming from your child probably has to do with his feelings, but it's no way to communicate if he eventually wants to be heard or respected. Don't cave in to Cancer's whiny ways. Illustrate what a "correct" kind of voice is, and insist that your little crab use it.

MANAGEMENT

Cancer, whether male or female, always gets pegged with the "Mommy" label. In childhood, this usually manifests as your child taking care of little animals or a colony of ants. As she grows, the skills that are learned in these childhood activities will be applied to the art of management. Cancer has incredible instincts, and because she "just knows" what other people need and want, this child can usually bring balance to an organization as well as the feeling that each individual within it is respected and liked.

FAVORITE THINGS

SING THESE SONGS WITH YOUR CANCER CHILD	› **"All Through the Night":** Gives baby Cancer an idea all will be okay.	› **"Over the River":** A Trip to Grandma's? YES!	› **"Itsy Bitsy Spider":** A song of true survival.
WATCH MOVIES LIKE THIS WITH YOUR CANCER CHILD	› *Charlotte's Web:* Saving the pig and the spider's offspring? Classic Cancer stuff.	› *Paulie:* All the love, mutual support, and a tearful reunion will reinforce Cancer's belief in true family values.	› *Homeward Bound:* Chance, the little bulldog in the film, finds something a Cancer always cherishes—a home.
PLAY THESE GAMES WITH YOUR CANCER CHILD	› **Jump Rope:** Cancer loves old-fashioned stuff, and this game gets your child moving.	› **Stickball:** Teaches tradition, following the rules, and hanging tough.	› **Mother May I?:** Cancer loves making Mother-ish decisions.
READ THESE BOOKS, RHYMES, AND FAIRY TALES TO YOUR CANCER CHILD	› *The Swiss Family Robinson:* A testament to the power of family.	› **"There Was an Old Lady Who Lived in a Shoe":** Cancer's love of children taken a step too far.	› **"The Snake and the Crab":** Addresses Cancer's critical tendencies and encourages self-examination.
TREAT YOUR CANCER CHILD TO THESE FOODS	› **Whole-Grain Bread:** Not to be overdone, but good comfort food.	› **Water:** The basic stuff. Cancer needs lots of it.	› **Melons:** Sweet and another good source of hydration.

✳ LITTLE CHALLENGES ✳

Your Cancer child's sensitivity might appear to be a good thing or a difficult matter, depending on your view. In any event, it does present a challenge for you as a parent. When the sound of crying emanates from the playroom, it's usually going to be your Cancer child who's doing it. There will be times, of course, when Cancer is injured or frightened; but there will be just as many incidences when he gets his feelings hurt. If you take the parental path of teaching that life contains certain elements of reality, you'll have to be objective about the way you judge each situation. Cancer will be wounded, of course, if your judgment comes down in favor of the other side, but you'll be teaching a lesson that he will need to learn in order to survive. Everyone in the world is *not* going to tiptoe around each and every mood. Cancer must learn to grow a thick skin and use that protective shell. This can be taken to extremes, though, and you'll find out about that when you're the one to hurt Cancer's feelings! The retreat your little crab makes into his shell can sting worse than the most vile and violent temper tantrum.

✳ DISCIPLINE ✳

Yes, your little Cancer is tender and docile, but she can and will do some "wrong" in early childhood. Most of the time, this will entail matters dealing with self-indulgence. Although your crab is sensitive, she is also somewhat impulsive. You might not want your baby to touch the pot of macaroni and cheese bubbling on the stove, but don't turn your back! Your Cancer often assumes you know far less than she does. After all, who's the *real* nurturer in this relationship?

Cancer might not have a very varied repertoire when it comes to resisting punishment, but that ultra-sensitivity will be put to use in various attempts to manipulate you into administering the lightest possible sentence. Cancer responds best to being isolated in a time-out type of situation, but you must never threaten your Cancer child without following through. Once Cancer loses respect for you, it's all over. Not only does Cancer have very sensitive emotions, your child also has a line on what upsets you! She will point out your flaws and insult you in attempts to show her dominance. Before you're done, even you'll be wondering who the parent is. Be consistent, strong, and predictable, and your Cancer baby will grow to be honest, accountable, and self-assured.

CANCER'S BABY STYLE

Cancer has a very practical and old-fashioned sense of style. Food stains can be a problem as this child really gets into food, often quite literally! That's why you want to stick to clothing that's easily washable. Cancer will enjoy dressing up, but only for really special occasions. Most of the time comfort will be favored over style.

GIRLS: She might like ruffles and lace or she may prefer soft, casual clothes that aren't too "pretty." Much depends on whether she plays mainly with boys or girls. She'll want to blend in and look like everyone else.

BOYS: Cancer boys won't be very trendy and will prefer to wear clothing that's not much different than what you might have worn as a child. He really does aspire to become the boy next door that everybody loves!

CANCER'S ENVIRONMENT

Cancer's nesting style is anything but neat. There will usually be clutter of some sort because Cancer has such a tough time letting go of things. Leave room for a large collection of toys, but help Cancer out by ensuring that there's a place to put it all.

CALMING CANCER

Cancer children are tender and sensitive, and yes, they do cry a lot. Sometimes it's because the world is too noisy, too cold, or too hot. Cuddling your child may work rather well, but if this doesn't work there could be tummy troubles. Cancer babies have notoriously nasty digestive problems because of the stomach's association with Cancer's ruler, the moon. As the child's moods go, so does the tummy!

Always be sure to burp your baby before bedtime. If she doesn't get all the air out before lying down, you'll be off to a bad start. Also, feed your little Cancer in a quiet and peaceful environment. Little crabs startle easily and can be frightened by sudden or loud noises. Even the sound of violence emanating from a TV in another room can stir up the wrong kinds of vibrations in her tender digestive system. A white noise machine to block out barking dogs and noisy neighborhood children might be a good addition to the nursery, too.

✳ STIMULATING CANCER ✳

Cancer always will respond well to being given the responsibility for taking care of someone or something. This child would love to have a baby sibling, of course, but if you're not up for that perhaps a relative or friend will fill the bill. Even Cancer boys love having the responsibility of making things or doing things for someone who needs their help. If you can't have a pet, maybe you can find ways to let your child learn to take care of animals at a local animal shelter or petting zoo. Here are some toys that will be well-loved by Cancer:

- **Stuffed Pets:** Always give Cancer something to cuddle with.
- **Baby Dolls or Fix-It Tools:** For Cancer to exercise domestic skills.
- **Kitchen Set:** Cancer will always want to "cook" for you.

✳ CANCER'S LEARNING STYLE ✳

Cancer learns through a series of sensations, and will associate those things that are committed to memory with what he could smell, hear, and sense at the time they were first learned. Cancer might learn how to read early because he will want to have another way of telling if things are all right. Security is always a big deal to Cancer, so tell your child early on that knowledge is power. A positive attitude in school will go a long way toward building a safe and secure life for your Cancer child.

PARENTING CANCER

If your sign is . . .

ARIES

You and your little crab are going to have a lot of things to work out, but you also have many things in common. First and foremost, you love one another. Always remember this, even when Cancer becomes uncooperative. You're usually very cheerful and outgoing, but that's not so for this baby. Cancer is a nurturer, but this child also requires a good deal of coddling. This can be awkward for you, because you're so direct and forceful about your physical expression. With a Cancer child, you'll need to pretend you're handling a delicate china doll, and this will apply to the baby's emotional make-up as well as his physical body.

You'll be an excellent teacher for Cancer, and will know how to teach your baby how to be "tough" enough to survive in the world. Meanwhile, your child will teach you about patience and how to become sensitive enough to sympathize with his feelings. Rather than push Cancer into rough sports and competitive situations, let your little crab show you the value of nurturing and calming down the savage beast that lurks in all of us. Watch your child handle a pet, even a large and powerful dog, and you'll see this magic take place.

TAURUS

You'll adore having your Cancer in the house. The infant's gentle movements and sweet personality will mold right into the peaceful home into which you've welcomed this little one. You might not believe, though, just how sensitive this child is. The first and slightest hint of your disapproval can provoke a river of tears. This child is very self-motivated, and your priorities won't always match. You both like to protect people, but your way of providing security is through material things, while Cancer needs security on a very emotional level. Your Cancer will push you to get more in touch with his emotions, and maybe even your own!

While you'll be very happy when your Cancer child does exactly what you want, you may not know what to do when he doesn't act the way you would predict. Cancer's tiny finger will still stay out of the electric socket just as surely if you pull your baby away gently as it would if you were to use more dramatic force. Cancer won't stand for being bullied, and if you want to assert your authority without creating an adversarial dynamic in your relationship, your best bet is to communicate with Cancer, whenever possible, with the kind of gentleness that he's likely to display to you.

GEMINI

You and your little Cancer will have a strange, yet easy relationship. The two of you have a totally different way of seeing the world, but because you're coming from two different places, you can maintain a nice exchange right from the beginning. The first thing you need to know, though, is just when you think you've done more than enough cuddling and coddling, Cancer will need much more. This is a very "touchy-feely" child, who will cling to you long after you figure she should have crawled off to see what's happening in the next room.

You'll easily be able to look out for Cancer, because you're always thinking ahead. Cancer, on the other hand, has instincts that are based on feelings. Just having this child in your life may open up a gateway to your own emotions. For one thing, identifying with Cancer's emotions will help you manage the child's needs more efficiently. You could, for example, stave off one of those long crying spells if you're just a little more sensitive to what your baby needs, including far less stimulation than you might think is possible.

CANCER

It's wonderful that you have a child with your exact same sun sign! Certainly you'll understand one another well, and you'll love playing the same games with

Cancer that you so enjoyed while you were growing up. That will be the case most of the time, but you'll also need to be prepared for some "curve balls" that your fellow crab might throw your way.

What can be so different about the two of you, you might ask? You may have forgotten what it's like to be a little Cancer. By now, you've grown to be a person who likes to take care of others, while your crab is still at the stage where she wants to be taken care of . . . all of the time! It might be hard to break your child of this neediness, because you do want to use your awesome nurturing abilities to solve every problem and prevent stress and tears. Still, you'll have to let your little Cancer do what you did, and that is to learn by example! From the beginning, show your Cancer child that while you love him unconditionally, you have your limits. This way, you'll help your Cancer child set limits and grow a strong outer shell, too.

LEO

Your gentle and adorable Cancer has fallen into the best possible set of arms! While Cancer seems to wants a lot of coddling, and needs as much or more than other children, your natural parenting energy fosters strength and confidence, which is invaluable for this little crab. Your Cancer baby will cry a lot, but the best thing to do isn't to dismiss or ignore the crying. You can be with your Cancer child, yet show him that everything is all right and there is no need to worry! A BabyBjörn or another kind of baby carrier that allows the baby to be close to your body will allow you to console the child as you go about your business—literally illustrating that there isn't a problem and nothing to cry about.

It may not seem as though you're giving your little Cancer what he needs all the time, even from his perspective. Remember that parenting is a long-term process, and what counts in the end is that you've created a self-sufficient young adult. Your grown-up Cancer will thank you for doing what you do.

VIRGO

This little one will indeed seem perfect in every way to you—everything you ever imagined you would see in a tiny infant. Indeed, baby Cancer is gentle and sweet, kind and generous. Your baby will smile up at you to let you know how much he looks to you for help and guidance. Remember this as baby Cancer begins to grow because your child isn't going to always be as precise or as sensible as you are. Your little crab is motivated by emotions, and will constantly remind you that feelings mean more than things, practices, or procedures. You might be more than a little bit maddened by the way your Cancer child keeps toys and clothing. There is usually total disarray that makes no sense to you at all! Work with Cancer on building better structure, but don't be overly critical. If you want to motivate Cancer, shell out compliments rather than corrections. Cancer is always anticipating your reactions, and if he expects disapproval he could develop a sense of shyness. Teach this gentle child to ground those big ideas to the earth through encouragement and support, and you'll raise a strong and responsible person you can be proud of!

LIBRA

You'll love holding your little Cancer in your arms. This baby will be so quiet and sweet, with an intensity that exudes love and loyalty, yet you might also sense that she is more than a little bit needy. You'll have to forget about looking your best from time to time, so you can tend to this baby's desire for reassurance. If you want to help this little crab stay away from being so nervous, give her a lot of physical contact at the outset. Although you might prefer to convey your love through words and gestures, Cancer needs to "feel" you.

As baby Cancer grows, the two of you will see eye to eye on most occasions, because you both like a lot of variety in life and enjoy the excitement of beginning new projects. Take your little Cancer to the museum with you or at least display some paintings or pictures that will help your child appreciate the fine arts. Creative outlets for Cancer's emotions are a must! You'll want to foster these activities and maybe even participate in them as well. Give Cancer all your love and even more affection than you think you should, and you'll be providing your child with the strength and appreciation he needs.

SCORPIO

You and your Cancer will have a very easy time relating because you totally get where this emotionally oriented child is coming from. You share this way of "just knowing" what other people feel, but you might not really like the way Cancer is so straightforward about demanding your constant attention. You aren't the kind of parent who will let your little one get away with undesirable behavior, so you'll want to get your child to soothe himself more easily. Rather than resorting to leaving him to cry in the crib (which translates to Cancer's psyche as being totally abandoned) you can get creative. Once your child is old enough to understand, ask him to "take care" of a stuffed animal or hold something for you. This will awaken Cancer's nurturing instinct and demonstrate how much fun it is to think outside his own needs.

There will be times when you'll have to administer discipline, of course, and when this comes up you should be as direct as possible. Let Cancer know when he is doing something dangerous or disruptive, but let your little crab know you will forgive transgressions, too. If you resort to ignoring this child, he will become deeply wounded on an emotional level—and you're both too sensitive for that!

SAGITTARIUS

You might not know what to do with your little crab right away, but you'll figure it out. This child is very sensitive and emotional, and well . . . you're not! This can be a good thing, though. Cancer needs to learn the rest of the world isn't going to waste time tiptoeing around her feelings. At the same time you'll have to become somewhat less brazen about saying what you think, especially if it sounds like you're criticizing this self-conscious child. Cancer children absorb what is said to them and process it very deeply, even in infancy. Part of the mutual learning process you'll go through while parenting the Cancer baby will entail becoming your own best editor.

While your Cancer child will like to play, you can't always assume that you'll be amused by the same activities. Throw any inhibitions you might have out the window and let Cancer take you to a tea party or a classroom filled with favorite stuffed animals. Cancer can learn to love sports, but such things must be introduced gradually and gently. This child is very delicate, physically and mentally, and it will be your job to help your little crab develop a little bit of a hard exterior shell.

CAPRICORN

You and your Cancer child will get along quite well, for some surprising reasons. You'll dote on her because of the tender way she takes in all the wonder in the world—including traditions and structures of organization—and does all she can to fit in with them. You'll also notice, though, how hypersensitive your Cancer is. The slightest foreign noise can set off a tirade of terror and you might spend more than one sleepless night trying to convince your Cancer child that "it was only a dream."

Your Cancer child admires your strength and confidence, and will develop these easily, as you provide an ideal role model. Let your little crab watch you organize an activity, play the role of manager, and climb the ladder of success. Your motivation is usually to provide a safe and secure place for your family to live, and no one will appreciate that more than your Cancer child! Be gentle with discipline, but don't spare corrections when they're needed. This child will try to get away with misbehavior and will often generate reasons for you to pay more attention. You can circumvent this by spending as much time as you can holding, watching, and listening to your Cancer.

AQUARIUS

You and the little Cancer you have in your life see the world in very different ways. That's why you're going to have to work extra hard at getting your child to avoid acting purely on emotion. There is more to life than the way a person feels, and in fact you hardly think about your own emotional life at all. Not logical by nature, your Cancer child processes everything through his emotional impressions and will have instincts that you might only wish you could develop.

You'll have to extend yourself a lot further than you expected in order to make your Cancer child feel safe and secure. If you're tired of holding the baby, go into a rocking chair and stay together a little longer. If Cancer seems fearful of a monster in the closet, spend whatever time it takes to show and convince your child that it isn't really there. Cancer will come to trust you and adore you more with every effort you make to show him that everything really *is* going to be all right.

PISCES

You'll love rocking your little Cancer for hours and holding that soft little bundle ever so close to you while he sleeps. As your Cancer child grows, though, you're going to have to come out of your dream world and live up to your little one's expectations. The Cancer child needs to have parents who will be solid and consistent, which means that you can't let bedtime slide because your child is having a good time or let Cancer eat "just potatoes" because that's what he likes. Even though you might think Cancer wants you to *give* in, the truth is Cancer is looking to you to provide a safe place for him to *grow up* in.

You'll need to discipline Cancer, and the best way will be usually through letting him know how the "bad" deeds could hurt people. Before Cancer becomes verbal, you'll have to move him away from any kind of danger, or prevent him from hitting you or anyone else by gently demonstrating that no matter how strong baby Cancer might like to be, you're still stronger. In the end, knowing someone is protecting him will help your little crab build a strong and noble character.

CHAPTER 5

Leo:

The Dramatic Star

BORN BETWEEN: July 22–August 21
RULING PLANET: The Sun
EXALTED PLANET: None needed! The sun has more than enough "oomph" to energize this sign!
COLOR: Orange and Gold
GEMSTONES: Citrine, Sardonyx

WHEN SUMMER IS AT ITS HEIGHT and all is lush and warm and wonderful is when Leo chooses to be born. Leo is a *fire* sign, and because the month of Leo is the middle of the season, Leo is *fixed*, that is to say very determined to have things go her way. You'll notice right away that your little Leo is rather dramatic about showing you what she wants. In fact, this baby is dramatic about everything! From the time you first hold your Leo, you'll know you have someone very special in your arms. Leo is symbolized by the lion, "king" (and "queen") of the jungle; so that could be why your child seems to exude this certain regal air. Will you be forced to deal with a problematic prima donna for the rest of your parenting life? Only if you fail to give Leo the leadership she needs to rein in some of her self-centered nature, which will help your Leo baby can earn the respect she so desperately craves.

Leo children don't merely ask for things; they demand them. Fortunately, they are very personable and cute, and usually quite striking. You'll recognize your Leo child's mane of thick and beautiful hair, whether she is born with it or it develops it over time. Leo requires a lot of physical activity, but will engage in it more willingly when it isn't merely your idea. As you may be able to tell, this child will make an attempt to seize authority at every opportunity, which is why it's so important for you to establish your guidelines early and always take charge. If Leo doesn't sense that you are strong enough to protect the entire family, she will constantly try to take charge of the operation. That should be enough reason for you to exercise your parental privileges without prejudice; this will also bring out your little Leo's biggest talent: warm-hearted leadership.

✳ YOUR LEO BOY ✳

A little bit demanding and very dynamic, your Leo boy wants to be noticed. Short of standing up in his crib only wearing a diaper and beating his chest, Leo will drop several hints a day that you should be telling him that he's cute, strong, and smart. You'll have to watch your boy when he plays around other children because he'll tend to appoint himself lord and master rather quickly! Most of the children will allow him to do this because he does have this way about him that lets the rest of the kids know he's the one who's got it all together. Don't try to stop him from taking his rightful place among his peers, but do monitor his activities to ensure that he always lets others take their turns.

The other thing you need to watch about your Leo boy's social behavior is that he doesn't wind up doing all the work for everybody else. Leo really does feel responsible for his friends, and inside he just wants to bring out the best in each of them. If he takes over too often and too much, though, he'll wind up being the one who's bullied into cleaning up after everyone.

Teach your Leo boy that he can be the leader most of the time, but that good leaders respect the talents of the people they work with and let everyone contribute. Also, you must always act with conviction and consistency when you're leading your little Leo boy through his infancy and early childhood because your lion will have to learn the difference between using his talents and showing what he can do—and "showing off." Leo boys will be especially prone to taking on the role of "class clown" because it's an easy way to get other people's attention. Rather than allowing this to happen, give your Leo boy an outlet for his thespian and comedic talents. He'll enjoy role-play with a puppet theater you set up in your home, or he could even show the kind of commitment that it takes to engage in a children's theater group. Seeing performances will be just as valuable as attending them, so make sure he gets a taste of what performing is and comes to realize early on that there's way more to it than goofing around so everybody looks at him.

✳ YOUR LEO GIRL ✳

Your Leo girl might not seem very delicate at all, and that's because she truly isn't! Her femininity is the kind one feels emanating from a very strong matriarch. Maybe one day, your entire family will refer to her as "she who must be obeyed," but while she is growing up under your protective watch, she must be the one who is giving deference to your wise and well-thought-out plans.

Yes, this means you must be on your toes with your little Leo girl more than you might have planned. While it seems to be appropriate in a day and age when parents are so conscious of empowering little girls, you might find your little Leo girl came born with the assumption that she can do anything she wants! If anything, you will have to encourage your Leo girl not to bowl over her friends. Her cute way of taking charge can all too easily become domineering.

One of the best things you can do for your Leo girl is put her in situations where she must deal with children of both sexes. For one thing, she needs to learn from males as well as females about cooperation and dominance. For another, she'll enjoy being around boys because they will, on the whole, be assertive and direct, the way she is. The other "must" for a little Leo is a plentitude of opportunities to be on stage. Whether as a dancer, a musician, an actor, or an announcer, Leo thrives on being in the spotlight. This is an important skill for her, as her main motivation is to be a leader. As she grows, you'll notice she is easily elected to positions of "power" and this is something that comes second nature to her. The difficult moments might come when she doesn't get to be the one in charge, and that's when you can step in to tell her that sometimes she will have to take her turn, and follow the leader the same way she would want everyone to follow her.

✳ TALENTS AND AFFINITIES ✳

DRAMATIC ARTS

Leo children excel at acting out dramatic roles. Not only is this a very productive way to develop presentation skills, grace, and the courage to speak in public, it's a useful alternative to allowing the Leo child to create drama in real life. Leo lives life to the fullest, and if there's not something exciting to act out about, Leo will configure situations that you will probably want to avoid.

LANGUAGE

Leo will seize on opportunities to learn how to speak. Although not very agile with words, Leo values them as a way of getting people to pay attention to what he wants to convey. Your Leo baby's first word isn't likely to be "Mama" or "Dadda," though. Because of your Leo baby's desire to build up a legend about himself, Leo's first word is most likely to be "Me."

PUBLIC SPEAKING

Leo is an attention-getter, and it's always best when this gregarious child has ample opportunities to stand up in front of an audience. Your child will be a great narrator, moderator, or emcee throughout elementary school and perhaps into adulthood. Foster Leo's talent by letting your little lion give you little "speeches," perhaps on the topic of why there should be more mirrors placed at Leo's eye level.

✳ LITTLE CHALLENGES ✳

Leo is such a charmer, but not everyone will see your child's outgoing personality and strident manner as a positive thing. At times, you will also wonder if maybe you told Leo "good job!" a few too many times. Leo is a legendary self-admirer, and this can lead to your child developing a larger-than-average ego. To some degree, you won't be able to stop Leo from being self-assured, and you wouldn't want to! Still, you will need to make sure that your child has consideration for the needs of others, and teach Leo that although it's important to love oneself, it's even more crucial to take care of those who need our help.

If you instill this attitude at an early age, you'll be able to forestall many of the classic Leo issues—bullying, throwing tantrums, and acting out like a prima donna. However, you would have rare success if you were to make it the whole way through Leo's childhood without confronting at least one of these behavior patterns. When you do, it's important that you teach Leo to stay within her boundaries. Once you do, your child will realize that these behaviors, no matter how tempting they are, won't get him anywhere.

✳ DISCIPLINE ✳

You have to be at least as strong and just as persistent as your little lion if you expect to discipline this child. As a baby, of course, there's little that Leo can do that is "wrong." Still, if you see that your child is about to touch something dangerous or forbidden, act with swiftness and conviction. Leo isn't particularly impulsive, but can often assume that what you say isn't really true. For instance, your Leo child might not believe the stove is "hot" until he gets near enough to touch it. Fortunately, Leo will probably stop short of putting a hand or a small stuffed toy in the oven; but it always pays to watch what Leo is up to, because your child's over-confidence can often lead to trouble.

If you become convinced Leo has deliberately done something that violates your rules, the punishment should double as a lesson that your Leo baby isn't the center of the universe. While Leo is still too young to do community service, consider getting your little Lion to do a job around the house. Even a toddler can "sweep" the floor or clean up toys that are dumped in the wrong places. Give Leo purposeful work that teaches him the value of putting effort into something that's good for the community—even when said community is just your household!

FAVORITE THINGS

SING THESE SONGS WITH YOUR LEO CHILD

> **"Twinkle Twinkle Little Star":** Leo will take a bow!

> **"Golden Slumbers":** Imagining what gold sleep must be like relaxes Leo.

> **"The Lion Tamer Song":** Not a bad way to let Leo know there are hoops to be jumped through!

WATCH THESE MOVIES WITH YOUR LEO CHILD

> *The Lion King:* What it really means to be King— or Queen.

> *The Cat in the Hat:* A feline take on Leo's "can do" attitude.

> *How to Train Your Dragon:* Leo is sure to love this story of taming a threat through love and leadership.

PLAY THESE GAMES WITH YOUR LEO CHILD

> **King of the Hill:** Of course!

> **Queenie, Queenie, Who's Got the Ball?:** A little lesson in the humility a regent needs in order to rule well.

> **Charades:** Even as a toddler, Leo will love acting out "big tree."

READ THESE BOOKS, RHYMES, AND FAIRY TALES TO YOUR LEO CHILD

> *King Arthur and His Knights:* Leo will be fascinated by this story of royal adventure.

> **"Old King Cole":** It can be good to be King—as well as daunting.

> **"The Boy Who Cried Wolf":** Here's what happens when you want too much attention.

TREAT YOUR LEO CHILD TO THESE FOODS

> **Carrots:** The color could draw Leo right into the vitamins.

> **Pineapple Juice:** Sweet and special—like your Leo baby.

> **Oranges:** The citrus flavor and texture will tantalize your Leo child.

LEO'S BABY STYLE

Do they make gold lamé diaper covers? If so, your baby Leo would wear one with panache. Leo has a very flashy style that always makes a statement, but never looks tacky while it does so. Favorite colors in clothes are red and orange, and for Leo girls—bright pink.

GIRLS: She'll be into Mommy's stilettos before she has even taken her first step in bare feet. She'll be after your reddest lipstick, too! Try not to let her be too precocious in her style.

BOYS: He'll want it to be dress up day every day when he starts nursery school. In the meantime, let him wear the superhero T-shirt two days in a row if it lets him feel like he stands out from the crowd. Or he may be even more blatant about his perceived royalty and don a regal purple robe!

LEO'S ENVIRONMENT

Leo will find utter silence to be unnatural. It might be a good idea to pipe in music or ambient sounds when you set up the nursery. In terms of décor, Leo will enjoy being surrounded by lots of color and large shapes. If you can find appropriate fixtures that feature a sunburst, Leo will be very pleased with them. Light will be soothing to Leo, too, so don't keep the nursery window blinds shut all the time.

CALMING LEO

Leo can become quite fierce when she cries for something, as well as amazingly persistent. Leo may be prone to having cramps in the chest area that affect breathing and digestion. Relax these by encouraging Leo to open up her arms as wide as she can.

To get her to go to sleep, just provide a steady (if boring) routine that signals, without exception, that it's time to turn off the lights and go to sleep. Give her something to hold on to as soon as Leo shows interest in a cuddly toy or favorite blanket. You can use this object as a signal that it's time for you to leave the royal chambers.

✳ STIMULATING LEO ✳

Little Leo's like toys that are brightly colored and exciting to play with. Try these toys:

- **A set of plush balls** with bells and bright colors.
- **Stuffed animals and puppets** that encourage role-play.
- **A baby drum** to let Leo play out that inner animal.

✳ LEO'S LEARNING STYLE ✳

Leo's biggest problem is learning how to listen. Although Leo can be quite successful in school, it takes teachers who are strong enough to manage Leo and who also have the knowledge and integrity that your lion will respect. You will have to be very judicious when it comes to choosing the right schools for this child. Leo is not the kind to just jump in and blend in with everybody else. Your Leo baby *isn't* "everybody else," and will spend most of his young life finding ways to be an outstanding student and citizen.

PARENTING LEO

If your sign is . . .

ARIES

Holding your lion must be a big thrill, and in case you didn't notice, it's likely that your little Leo will continually remind you how special it is, in some way or other. You'll marvel at how brave and brazen your child is, and while all this is wonderful, if you're not careful, baby Leo could wind up running your household!

When it comes to attention, you're usually happier when it flows in your direction and people put their focus on you. Yet your sympathy for Leo might push you to spend most of your time tending to Leo's every move, emotion, and whim. Of course it's appropriate for you to take care of your baby's basic needs, but you'll have to be strong if you expect to avoid doing nothing *but* making sure baby Leo is happy. Perhaps one of the best lessons you can teach one another is that it isn't possible to have 100 percent of the attention 100 percent of the time. Funny enough, you'll be teaching Leo a lesson that you might have had to learn sometime in your life, and you'll be a terrific teacher!

TAURUS

You and Leo will make a really cool parent-baby match. While your child is far more dramatic and demonstrative than you are, he is every bit as determined and tenacious. Raising this child is going to teach you a lot about how hard it is to be with someone who is (like you can be at times) rather unmovable. This is very likely to inspire you to become more flexible, or at least teach your Leo how he can be easier to get along with.

You'll admire Leo's leadership faculties and will foster these with pleasure and pride. You might act as Leo's sounding board a lot of the time, and it's important to know when Leo really has to have your full attention and when you need your privacy or must direct your focus on something or someone else. Your admiration for this child could give you a tendency to defer to Leo's wishes somewhat too often. When Leo is claiming more territory than you allow, give your child guidelines about when it's okay to interrupt, and stick to them. The best gift you can give this child is an unwavering moral compass that helps Leo choose, no matter the pressure applied, to do the right thing.

GEMINI

The fact is you might not know what to do with your little Leo! Where you may tend to want to let your child explore the world as an independent agent, Leo has a long list of demands for you to consider. When you think your lion is satisfied with the amount of time you've spent together, she will insist you read another story, go on another walk, or play one more game.

You may not like to have someone watching over you all the time, but Leo has other ideas. The good news is you can read Leo like a book, but that's also the bad news! You'll know when your Leo baby's cries are the real thing, and when Leo is using them simply to get your attention. Still, this child's dependency upon you might demonstrate the importance of being more attentive and giving up at least some small part of your freewheeling lifestyle. Maybe you can keep up with at least some of your friends electronically, while baby Leo naps nearby. Leo will appreciate your storytelling ability, and will develop the art of conversation under your careful tutelage.

CANCER

You'll get hours of entertainment out of your little Leo and will want to coddle and protect your child. While there will be times when you notice you're learning important lessons from your little one, on the whole you'll be the one who dominates the relationship—because you're the one who *is* the parent!

Don't let Leo become overly demanding. You have instincts that allow you to know exactly when your baby is trying to fool you into believing there's some sort of baby-related emergency. When Leo starts to put on a show, don't play into it. Your indifference may get through to Leo and will prevent your baby from becoming a demanding little dictator. Teach Leo instead to be strong, courageous, and honest. These virtues will serve your child well for an entire lifetime.

LEO

Your little Leo has no idea what kind of arrangement the cosmos has made for the two of you! Just like you, your child will believe that she should be the center of attention, but because you've already learned why that isn't always possible, you'll probably confront her with this reality at the outset. You have a magnificent talent for parenting, but because your sign is closely aligned with the sun it isn't the coddling kind. You'll love teaching your Leo child to be strong and courageous, while you also administer praise in amounts that are properly attenuated to get your Leo baby to strive to meet expectations.

If you get frustrated with anything about living with this little "mini-me" of yours, it might be the competition the child will give you for the attention of your spouse and other relatives. You'll probably find yourself constantly reminding little Leo how hard it is to live with a person who's constantly trying to get attention— and maybe you'll learn a lesson or two about the same issue, too. As your baby grows, you have the potential to develop even further as a human being. That, perhaps, is the coolest thing about parenting there is!

VIRGO

From the start, the amount of drama your little one brings into your life will be fun, if a little disruptive. Even when there is simply a soiled diaper to change, your baby Leo will act out the condition of being wet or dirty with each little cry and gesture! You'll get a kick out of your baby, but you'll also wonder if the universe isn't playing a little joke by sending this live wire into your otherwise orderly life.

There's a reason you've been put together. First and foremost, you must teach Leo to focus that awesome energy on doing something productive. Then you can also look to Leo for some lessons on how to be a lot more easygoing than you're prone to be. Leo's dramatic talents, and the antics they produce, are going to give you plenty of reasons to want to pull your hair out. Yet when you open up to welcome a little bit of randomness into your life, you will let in warmth and laughter you might have never known had you not welcomed this dynamic little child into your heart and home.

LIBRA

Raising your Leo will call upon you to bring out your most courageous traits in order to keep your baby's considerable energies contained. Your lion is probably no more egocentric than you are, but this little one is far more overt about putting herself out there and in front of just about everyone else! You have the perfect combination of talents, as well as the sense of balance and justice, that Leo needs to see in order to bring that brash and bossy little personality into line.

You don't have to get harsh with your child in order to get your point across. Because your Leo will thrive on applause and approval, when you fail to lavish these things on your baby, Leo will get a strong message. Even more than you do, Leo wants to know that he is "okay" with you—and when it seems like that might not be the case, that courageous, tyrannical little lion can turn tail and run scared. Try to be as direct with Leo as you can, and don't keep your child guessing. Give your Leo the same kind of reassurance that you yourself need.

SCORPIO

You're going to have a lot of fun raising the little bundle of joy that is your Leo. You have a wisdom that sees right through this baby's brave and domineering act, and you won't allow him to manipulate you under any circumstances. Boundaries, circumstances that produce life lessons, and a determination to teach your lion to channel his energies into useful and productive activities will be the best things you can give to your Leo baby.

If there's any difficulty that you have to overcome while you're parenting little Leo, it will be to reconcile the difference between each of your levels of emotional IQ. You, of course, are at the high end of the scale. If there's something wrong with your Leo child, you'll know before he even begins to fuss. Leo is nowhere near as sensitive as you are and the sooner you accept this, the better; once you do you'll be able to get through the process of containing and admiring this very dynamic child without as much risk of getting your feelings hurt.

SAGITTARIUS

You'll bounce your little Leo in your arms and figure you've found your new little teensy-tiny best friend! You share the passion of fire with Leo, and the two of you are both dynamic and outgoing. There will be a lot of laughter in your household, right from the beginning. Even as an infant, Leo will get your sense of humor and giggle right along with you.

That said, you must be careful of creating too much of a peer-type relationship with your Leo child. Leo has the tendency to take over in situations even when you're the one who's supposed to be the authority figure. This is something your little baby cannot help, because she has strong leadership abilities and, naturally, wants to use them! As much as you'd love to be able to act as innocent and carefree as your child, that isn't your role here. Leo, like you, has strong primal instincts, and will try to dominate in almost every relationship. You must show your child that you're even wiser and stronger than you appear. Set rules, discipline your baby with love, but be firm! Then you will be doing all the best things for your Leo baby.

CAPRICORN

You and your Leo will have some initial difficulties seeing eye to eye, but ultimately, if you're patient, you'll be the beneficiaries of the best kind of parent-child relationship. The problem you must overcome is the way Leo seems to be confused about who the boss is in your household. Far from being complacent and compliant, your little lion will try to dominate you and your household, first by trying to set the schedule through demands for feeding and changing, and later with more disruptive activity.

You're going to have to be very firm with this baby, far more serious and unyielding than you think you need to be if you intend to establish your authority.

Once Leo realizes there's no possibility of usurping your authority, the two of you will get along great. You'll know how to get Leo to channel that "me first" energy into activities that develop leadership and compassion. While Leo works more with individuals and you envision the big-picture management view, the two of you have a lot to learn from one another and the potential to have a whole bunch of fun! Both of you very much want to bring out the best in others by shining the light of your stellar example.

AQUARIUS

You and your little Leo will have a lot of ups and downs throughout your relationship, but during your baby's infancy you'll want it to be as quiet, peaceful, and loving as possible. You'll enjoy nurturing your child through the early stages and will take care of his needs, but you'll also show Leo that there's more to the world than what's going on in his little bubble. You'll socialize your child by taking him with you while you run errands, and you'll encourage little Leo to share the sunshine that emanates from that little heart with everyone your baby meets.

As your little lion grows, though, he might not respond to you the way you would like. Leo is a very strong individualist and doesn't like to be told what he "must" do. You're going to have to negotiate—a lot! While you're thinking about what is best for the whole world, your Leo child is focused on his own development and success. You can be gratified that one day this will mean your child will spend time bringing out the best in other people. In the meantime, you're going to have to make sure your little Leo doesn't become a big, self-centered bully—and you're the best teacher your Leo child could ask for.

PISCES

You are very spontaneous, "loose" when it comes to your schedule, and exceedingly creative and imaginative. While Leo will appreciate these qualities in you, she will seek more predictability and routine than you might like. Despite this, you and your Leo will have a great deal of fun discovering one another. However, because you're so different it's going to be difficult to know what to do with this dynamic and courageous child at first. Just like all babies, little Leo needs love and a safe place in which to grow. To Leo, a safe place would be like a lion's den—enclosed, protected, and safe from the elements. This means you might have to adjust some things to allow Leo to feel this.

Leo might also try to walk all over you when he discerns that you aren't nearly as strong-willed as he is. You're going to have to do a quick study on the art of leadership, and get going with it right away! Something that might work for you—and your baby—is to study martial arts, even together! You'll learn a lot about self-empowerment, and your Leo child will have a safe place to be assertive and strong—and learn limits. Don't be afraid to ask for help when dealing with little Leo—you may need it!

CHAPTER 6

Virgo:

The Little Worker Bee

BORN BETWEEN: August 22–September 20
RULING PLANET: Mercury – The nighttime, more reserved, and discerning side
EXALTED PLANET: Mercury
COLOR: Leaf Green, Brown
GEMSTONES: Blue Sapphire, Malachite

THE TINY BABY YOU'RE HOLDING is sweet, wise, and very discerning. As your Virgo child grows, you'll notice how this clever little creature examines everything and then decides whether it should be kept or left to the side. Virgo is an *earth* sign, but is also *mutable*, which means your little Virgo is able to adapt to changing circumstances. Virgo must be performing some sort of service in order to feel good about being who he is. You'll notice how, from a very early age, your Virgo seems to make every move a purposeful one. There are good things about this and some that you'll need to help little Virgo improve upon.

Virgo is very good at performing small tasks and doesn't even look for your approval when they are completed. Your child will take great joy in being the one to sort all the shapes or stack all the rings in the proper order. "Order," as it happens, is also very important to your Virgo baby. To a Virgo, things are never "good enough" unless they're as near to perfect as possible. Although it's kind of nice to think your child will keep the house clean and avoid soiling every piece of clothing in the house, you have to try to set limits for little Virgo. In a constant pursuit of perfection, your Virgo child may begin to disapprove of his own imperfections to such a degree as to be self-destructive. If you notice phobias, obsessions, and other behavior ticks developing, address them immediately. Your Virgo baby needs constant reassurance that everyone makes mistakes!

Virgo takes in the world through the mind, constantly analyzing and sorting. A healthy Virgo will be critical at times, but for the most part will also be very exacting in the way he administers love, affection, and loyalty to you and the rest of the family.

✳ YOUR VIRGO BOY ✳

Many parents complain that their little boys are noisy, disruptive, and sloppy, but your young Virgo boy will be anything but. In fact, Virgo will be very much like a "little man" while growing up. He'll play with toys in sequence, put them away, and then go to the next activity without much fuss. He'll let you dress him when and in what you think is appropriate, and he'll do what you tell him to do the majority of the time.

You must be careful, though, that you don't do anything that makes him feel something is out of order. For Virgo, everything has a place. If you leave things lying around or if you fail to put his toys where he expects to find them, he could become a lot less compliant. In fact, he will tend to correct you and stop accepting your authority. Within reason, this can be cute, but if you let it go too far your little Virgo can become quite dictatorial. Also, the feeling that you don't know what you're doing will upset Virgo! These hard little workers can also become obsessive worriers. One chink in your parental armor and Virgo will assume that you're utterly unreliable. Then your little obedient "soldier" will appoint himself a five-star general. Suddenly, you'll be getting a constant stream of criticism. Emphatic strains of "No, Mommy!" or "Stop, Daddy!" will quickly morph into a stream of snide criticism if you're not careful to nip it in the bud as soon as it starts.

Your mission as a parent is to get a very important point across: No one and nothing can be perfect, so while it's nice to try to get things the way we want them, sometimes we have to accept imperfections so we can work on solving problems and moving forward. Your Virgo boy very much needs to learn this lesson, for the sake of his mental health—as well as yours! Give your Virgo boy some toys that accelerate this lesson. Building blocks (that ultimately fall down) or toys that help him use his considerable handiwork skills will be well-liked and highly instructional on more than one level.

✳ YOUR VIRGO GIRL ✳

Your Virgo girl will be extremely feminine, if not frilly. As a young infant, she'll appear to be very delicate. No one who peers into her stroller or carriage will ask, "Is it a boy or a girl?" because they'll already be able to tell; her fine features and gentle movements will exude the sweetness and affection that you always imagined when you thought of what a little baby girl would be. As your Virgo girl grows, she will continue to pay a great deal of attention to appearance. This will be less for the sake of glamour and more to strive for neatness and appropriateness. Virgo's zodiac symbol is "the virgin," and it refers to the vestal virgins who did service by tending to the fire during the early parts of their lives, and were then allowed to go forth, find mates, and start families. Still, the part of Virgo's being that can be characterized in the classical sense as "virgin" or pure seems to have stuck with most people born under this sign, both male and female. With that said, your Virgo girl will seem to embody it more obviously and fervently than her male counterpart.

You'll probably notice that your Virgo isn't big on having a lot of people around her. First, she must learn to trust her normal environment, including you and the way you play with her. Always be gentle with your Virgo girl, and don't make direct efforts to teach her how to be tough right away. Let her establish trust and then teach her to protect herself, both physically and emotionally. The best way to do this is to equip her with the simple knowledge that it's okay to tell when someone makes her feel uncomfortable. Her shyness will dissipate as she gets older, and her self-protectiveness will also become stronger, as long as you accept her for who she is and encourage her to follow her particular path.

Even though you might wonder why it's so important to her to take care of others, you must understand this is how she will interact with the world and eventually create a niche for herself in adulthood. Foster this by giving her plants to tend to or pets to clean up after. In time, she'll build confidence in herself because she is so capable of answering requests and fulfilling needs.

✳ TALENTS AND AFFINITIES ✳

ARTS AND CRAFTS

Your little Virgo will be extremely adept at putting little projects together. Both boys and girls will enjoy cutting, pasting, and stickers. Be prepared, though, for the little eruptions that can take place when things don't go as planned. An upside-down or misplaced picture of a favorite cartoon character can provoke a self-critical perception of utter failure.

LANGUAGE

Virgo is likely to be very precise about speech and reading. If you don't notice your little Virgo picking up words and phrases as fast as you think he should, consider breaking everything down to its elements. Virgo children need rules and structure in order for the world to make sense. Rather than relying on whole-language or rote memorization, you may have to teach phonics and delve into grammar at an early age.

GARDENING

Little Virgo hands like to make contact with the dirt. This might not make sense considering how hygienic many Virgo people can be, but earth is Virgo's element, and the act of growing an herb or flower garden can help put your little one in touch with those "roots." Even as a young toddler, your Virgo child can find solace in harnessing the power of the earth to help foster the growth of beautiful plants and flowers.

✳ LITTLE CHALLENGES ✳

Virgo's desire for perfection can be hard to understand, especially when you'd rather accomplish things fast than get them done "perfectly." This can range from getting Virgo to dress without fussing over little things like small stains and slightly loose shoelaces to arranging all the items on your child's plate to her satisfaction. While you might see these strong organizational tendencies as a big plus (and they can be!), you need to also guard against allowing your Virgo child to exercise them without limits.

Somewhere behind this seemingly earnest desire to do everything "right" lurks Virgo's true motivation: to gain and maintain control over her environment. Virgo will criticize you with just a look, and certainly with words as she gets older. For Virgo's own good as well as your own, you must put yourself in a higher position in the pecking order, and insist your Virgo child defer to it at all times.

It's important to know that there are some Virgo children who come to the realization they will never be "perfect," and they just give up on neatness and organization altogether. If your child doesn't seem to fit the Virgo prim and proper mold, then maybe this is what's going on. You must then be stricter about getting your child to bring order into her life. It can be a relief to have a Virgo child who's not so rigid, but without some sense of order and structure your Virgo will remain rudderless and insecure. As always, as a parent it's best to do what will provide your child with a helpful balance of self-love and generosity.

✳ DISCIPLINE ✳

How do you discipline a child who probably already over-disciplines himself? Even though your Virgo child might seem to be enforcing rules and pointing out violations on a regular basis, in fact, there will be times when this child simply gets out of line. When this happens, you must be ready to provide the overriding order and authority that your child is probably, on some unconscious level, asking you for.

Virgo must be taught the lesson that he isn't always the one in charge, and doesn't really know what's best for everybody involved. A good way to do this is to gently impose your will on your little Virgo. Let's say your child prefers walks or stroller rides to the park rather than going to the grocery store. Rather than giving your child a choice in the matter, simply announce what you are going to do, then do it. If Virgo objects, then you will have a bit of a battle of wills, and you had better win it!

Virgo will do what he can to aggravate and upset you, so the best way to react under this scenario, or any other that involves Virgo trying your patience, is to act detached, calm, and assertive. When you don't play into this child's game, Virgo won't have any control over you. This is probably the very best way to ensure that Virgo sees that there are rules and restrictions other than the ones he sets up for everyone else.

FAVORITE THINGS

SING THESE SONGS WITH YOUR VIRGO CHILD	❯ **"The Green Grass Grows All Around":** Horticultural happiness.	❯ **"Bingo":** Appeals to Virgo's tenacious attention span and detail orientation via knowing when not to clap.	❯ **"Jump Down, Turn Around":** All about the work of cotton picking.
WATCH MOVIES LIKE THIS WITH YOUR VIRGO CHILD	❯ *Antz:* The essential contribution of the worker to society in a nice movie.	❯ *Mary Poppins:* This musical tale of a lovable caretaker will appeal to Virgo's sense of order.	❯ *The Secret Garden:* Virgo will relate to the idea of taking a sad situation and turning it into something beautiful by doing something useful.
PLAY THESE GAMES WITH YOUR VIRGO CHILD	❯ **Cat's Cradle:** Great for developing manual dexterity.	❯ **Rock, Paper, Scissors:** Shows force isn't always the trump card.	❯ **Crazy Eights:** Virgo's Mercury-aided mind loves a good card game, especially when sorting is involved.
READ THESE BOOKS, RHYMES, AND FAIRY TALES TO YOUR VIRGO CHILD	❯ *The Wind in the Willows:* Everyone, everything, has a time and a place in this book.	❯ **"Old Mother Hubbard":** Appeals to Virgo's desire to be of service.	❯ **"The Ant and the Grasshopper":** The industrious one wins again!
TREAT YOUR VIRGO CHILD TO THESE FOODS	❯ **Whole-Wheat Pasta:** Virgo needs easy-to-digest and wholesome foods.	❯ **Pear Juice:** Plain, simple, yet very appealing.	❯ **Broccoli:** Virgo will eat healthy—and loves the color green.

✳ VIRGO'S BABY STYLE: ✳

Simple, neat, and prim is the only way to go with a Virgo. Keep your child comfortable, but also consider allowing Virgo to wear "nice" things. There will be occasional stains in any child's life, and when they happen they must be dealt with as soon as possible. Still, Virgo will prefer nice pants or a skirt to sloppy overalls or sweats.

GIRLS: This little princess will adore wearing little skirts and pretty shoes. She'll love those matching "just like me" sets that she can share with her favorite doll.

BOYS: He'll want to wear his dress-up clothes and may even inspire you to buy tuxedo-style Onesies. Still, plan on reinforced knees in his pants as he grows older and gets involved in digging and gardening.

✳ VIRGO'S ENVIRONMENT ✳

Virgo's environment should be as clutter-free as possible. Although you might not mind a few things laying around, your Virgo could possibly be psychically disturbed by disorder. If you have a Virgo baby who just won't stop crying, try cleaning up the area enough so there is more calm and order in the room. You might find this is all you need to do in order to keep your little Virgo nice and content.

✳ CALMING VIRGO ✳

In addition to keeping his quarters clean and neat, you can always calm your little Virgo by keeping him busy. During infancy, this might consist of having him grab your finger or handing him a rattle to play with. Later, if Virgo just won't hear any more about taking a nap, supply a busy-box type toy in the crib. The act of "work" can actually make your little Virgo more at peace with the world. Start preparing baby Virgo to take a rest long ahead of the actual bedtime or nap period. A steady, predictable routine is more important to a child like this than it is to most, so try to stick to it as much as possible.

✳ STIMULATING VIRGO ✳

Virgo will pay attention to the details, and there are a ton of toys that are sure to please. Start with some like these:

- **Puzzles:** Even as a baby, Virgo enjoys the intricate thought process of figuring out what pieces fit, and where.
- **Sewing and Fastening Toys:** Virgo loves to latch, unlatch, zip, unzip, and yes, even sew. Those fine motor skills develop in Virgo far faster than average.
- **Sandbox:** Just to shake your Virgo baby up, provide this opportunity to get "dirty." The shoveling and sifting tools will be a favorite, and you'll be amazed at how seriously your tot takes filling up a simple bucket.

✳ VIRGO'S LEARNING STYLE ✳

Virgo learns by making choices, and has a very stark sense of sorting things out. This can be wonderful later in life when your child becomes an ace accountant. As a child, though, you'll have to balance Virgo's "either/or" sense of the world by demonstrating the utility of using shades of gray. Present your child with a blackboard, an easel, and modeling clay as well as sorting toys and puzzles to help Virgo unleash crafts prowess and creativity.

PARENTING VIRGO

If your sign is . . .

ARIES

Raising little Virgo will seem like a no-brainer, especially when you note how mild-mannered she seems to be. This might change as your child begins to grow, however. This child won't respond well to your fast and furious lifestyle and will need a lot more tenderness than you naturally tend to show. You'll need to practice the art of quiet, and also employ yourself (or a maid) as a much better cleaner-upper.

You're going to have to deal with the way your little one insists on having certain things done in set ways without allowing him to run all over you. This will take patience over time, and you probably know this isn't your strong suit. Also, this child has a whole other way of socializing, and although you don't understand it you must allow your little Virgo to be the shy and retiring type until he develops more trust in other people.

When it comes to making rules, resist any temptation to reverse roles. Your Virgo needs your strong sense of independence and freedom to help him grow into a balanced, assertive, and secure adult one day.

TAURUS

You and little Virgo will be fast friends. Both of you see the value in being useful and practical, and you'll agree on most of your favorite activities. The difference between you and your Virgo child will be in the amount of time you spend on making yourselves feel good—and how. While you like to cater to your senses, your little Virgo feels better when she is making other people feel good.

This could become dangerous for your relationship, especially if you decide that you'd prefer your little Virgo to take care of you! This isn't appropriate, so stop yourself from asking this tyke to get you your glass from across the room. Virgo could also become very critical of you, and make you wonder which of you is the child. If this happens, you must inform Virgo that you're the one making the rules, and enforce them without becoming lenient.

At the same time, you have to let Virgo do *some* little things for you. Allow your child to make pictures or clay figures for you, or even bring you one of his favorite toys. The focus should be on building Virgo's self-esteem and developing his skills.

GEMINI

Although you're far more social and active than your Virgo child, the two of you have a lot in common. You share an affinity for the planet Mercury and the things it represents, such as communication, thinking, and coordination. You and Virgo have the idea of logistics hard-wired into your brains, so the early part of infancy with all the scheduling and structure will be easy for you to figure out. You'll probably fall on to a common wavelength without a problem.

As your little Virgo grows, however, there could be some difficulty when you try to make your social styles mesh. While you're anything but shy and retiring, Virgo doesn't tend to "work the room" the way you do. Rather than pushing your child to be like you it's important to accept that, although Virgo will have plenty of friends, she won't be the social butterfly you are. You can help Virgo see that most people are "safe" by setting the example of being outgoing and friendly. Still, you must let your Virgo child choose, within reason, the close circle of friends she will play with, from the sandbox to the college dorm.

CANCER

Your Virgo child will be easy to take care of, and the two of you will build a very solid relationship. You have a way of setting up just enough structure for your little Virgo without making it seem as though he has absolutely no control over his activities. You are a master of allowing children to be who they are, and in this case you can foster

Virgo's worker bee talents and organizational skills by putting him in charge of age-appropriate chores around the house.

Before you get to the point where this will make sense, though, you must first get through the early stages. The hardest part for you while you're raising Virgo will be creating the calm and uncluttered environment your Virgo child thrives in. You will need to throw away more things than you might want to just so Virgo can create a sense of neatness in his room. Also, don't be offended by Virgo's lack of sentimentality about having certain objects around. The first teddy bear and last lock of baby hair can be tossed aside the minute they are no longer useful. Fortunately, Virgo is less brutal about casting aside human beings, especially a loving and caring parent like you.

LEO

You and your little Virgo will be happy together as long as you realize your child is with you to learn certain things, but not to live under your "rule." The Virgo baby has definite ideas about what she needs, and will not hesitate to tell you, either through crying and fussing or in very strong words, what you're doing wrong. You might like people to think that you're not bothered when they disapprove of the things you do; but the fact remains that this child can make you feel very inadequate with just a look.

It's Virgo's job to study and then criticize, or at least that's what your child will believe. Until you set the record straight, and prove your confidence is far more than mere bravado, Virgo will continue to challenge you. You might be tempted at times to scare this baby off with a "roar," but this won't work very well. Although shy, Virgo remains skeptical of your abilities, at least until you prove them.

Bring out the best in your baby by being the leader without becoming a dictator and you'll gain the respect that you're after. You'll also do your Virgo the favor of giving him the tools he'll need to survive in the world, throughout childhood and beyond.

VIRGO

You and your Virgo will be very happy together because you tend to see things the same way. You know how to set up the household in a way that makes your little Virgo feel comforted and soothed as well as stimulated. However, you must be careful not to fall into the pattern of catering to every need your baby might have.

When you don't provide the strength and structure your baby needs, she might respond by acting out on feelings of insecurity and fear. This could lead to crying jags that seem to last an eternity. You must ensure that your own confidence in your abilities as a parent is strong and unwavering. If you're not sure what to do about a certain situation, then do the research. Ask an older relative or parent-peer what do if and when your baby seems to cry for no apparent reason.

You might want to begin on the journey of creating structure and comfort for baby Virgo by holding her more than you might think you should and ensuring she is wrapped in blankets that give that sense of being "held." This will make sense to you. After all, aren't you exactly the same way?

LIBRA

Your Virgo child will be surprisingly easy to get along with. This little one will appreciate and enjoy the way you add those pretty little touches to being a parent. The nice clothing and peaceful environment that you create for your little Virgo will feel calming and reassuring to your baby. These are essential elements for Virgo and you'll have no problem providing them at all.

As your child grows, though, the two of you may not see things the same way. Virgo babies must be in a constant state of "doing." You, on the other hand, are much happier when you're in a state of "just being." While it might be nice to have your Virgo child offering to fetch you things or help you pick up stuff around the house, you can't take this kind of role reversal too far.

It's crucial to develop a leadership role in your relationship with your Virgo child because your sometimes too-gentle approach could possibly leave Virgo feeling unstable and insecure. Always make sure your Virgo understands how much you appreciate his efforts to help you, but make it clear that you'll always be there to clean the messes and fight off the "dragons" that Virgo fears so intensely.

SCORPIO

You and your little Virgo will create an entertaining dynamic that your family members will probably enjoy watching. You probably already know how much you like to have control over what happens in your life, but now you have a baby with an equally intense desire to be the manager and director of all affairs!

It won't take long for you to establish dominance over your baby—in the most loving and embracing way, of course. It would be a shame, though, if you were to miss out on what the Virgo child has to teach *you!* Maybe you'll find it isn't always about digging deep into the well of emotions, especially with your little one. Rather than suffering from psychic damage as the result of another relative's remark about your little Virgo's hairstyle or favorite shirt, your child could be crying just because a diaper change is in order!

On some level, your Virgo child likes to see you squirm, so don't allow these small matters to erode your patience or your confidence. Give baby Virgo some of your tenacity and utmost faith in your capabilities, and your child will be almost as much of a powerhouse as you are!

SAGITTARIUS

You will be overjoyed at the arrival of your Virgo baby because this child will seem to have it all together from the beginning. Once you get settled into a daily routine, though, things could change a bit. Your Virgo might not always be as happy and easygoing as you are!

It's really important for you to enclose baby Virgo in an envelope of security and safety. Rather than strapping this tyke into a jogger stroller and running off to prep yourself for an upcoming 5K race, you might need to spend some time sitting still and holding the baby. Virgo must learn to trust you, and this will be quite a slow process. Try not to lose patience when your baby is afraid of the bath water, or traffic, or an approaching dog. Look at your mission as being one that alleviates this tender child's fears.

Once you accomplish this, and show by example that there's far less to fear than your Virgo child thinks, the two of you may enjoy doing some of the more rugged stuff that you really get into. In the meantime, you'll need to slow down and let baby Virgo catch up. Perhaps you can take a moment to stop and smell the flowers, too.

CAPRICORN

You'll love your little Virgo even more than you thought you would! The two of you will have so much in common, and even with control issues of his own your Virgo baby will defer to your capable leadership. If all parents of Virgo children could be like you, Virgos would all grow up with a healthy sense of self-esteem.

You have a special way of equipping your little one with the confidence it takes to face the world. Your calm, competent leadership encourages Virgo to follow you, yet also inspires your child to develop a strong spine and the faith it takes to reach for goals that might seem just a bit out of reach.

Sometimes little Virgo might get a little rebellious. This child, just as you do, seems to think he knows exactly what everyone should be doing at any given moment. Until your child grows up to be a responsible adult, though, you must teach the importance of succumbing to reality and authority, even when the methods being used don't seem to make as much sense as the ideas of your sensible, practical, and somewhat controlling little Virgo.

AQUARIUS

You and your little Virgo could have some issues from the beginning. You might find it hard to understand what possible kind of problem this child might be having, as you figure you've given baby Virgo food, shelter, clothing, and at least some comfort. The problem might indeed be that your child needs more coddling and reassurance. Virgo comes into the world certain that she knows how it "ought" to be, but she's sometimes very shy and afraid when it comes to trusting things the way they are.

Little Virgo will grow more assertive, and sometimes snide, when she senses that what you're focused on isn't terribly practical. Unless Virgo can find a "here and now" place to apply your ideas she will have little use for them. This little one needs to be shown there is more to life than gratifying the needs of individuals, and you'll be the perfect teacher for this lesson.

Get your little Virgo involved in community activities as soon as that becomes possible. Before that, read stories that involve the idea of doing for others on a grand scale. Virgo will always be down with being of help, but it will take a visionary like you to get Virgo to raise her head above the level of the grindstone.

PISCES

You'll adore your little Virgo, perhaps a little bit too much! While you'll be very good at creating a peaceful and nurturing environment for this nervous little child, you might need to work on your organization skills! Virgo needs regular times for everything and very few if any changes in the schedule that you set. Your freeform kind of attitude will make this baby feel insecure, and when that happens, your baby will cry.

You obviously can't change who you are, not even for your child, but you'll do well to create more structure in your life. Pay more attention to the clock and the calendar and keep track of what needs to be done from one moment to the next.

Once your Virgo child is assured that things will happen as predicted there will be far less fussiness and fewer sleepless nights.

Your little Virgo will benefit greatly from your ability to transcend hard, cold realities and delve into the world of magic and imagination. Despite the vast differences in your points of view, the two of you will be best friends for life—as long as you develop and maintain a strong sense of security that lets Virgo know you're always going to steer him in the right direction.

CHAPTER 7

Libra:

The Peaceful, Brainy Romantic

BORN BETWEEN: September 21–October 21
RULING PLANET: Venus – The artistic and justice-loving side
EXALTED PLANET: Saturn
COLOR: Pale Green, Pink, and Black
GEMSTONES: Opal and Watermelon Tourmaline

THIS BUNDLE OF BEAUTY THAT'S BEEN HANDED DOWN TO YOU at harvest time is born under the sign of the scales. Libra is an *air* sign, and as it begins the autumn season, it is *cardinal*, which gives Libra a desire for variety and action. The Libra baby has a very active mental life, and enjoys the beginnings of things the most. Libra craves perfect balance, peace, harmony, and beauty. This baby is naturally charming and very pleasant to be around. Full of smiles and quieter than the average infant, Libra's chief desire is to make others happy.

Libra is constantly taking stock and keeping score. While monitoring your every kiss to see if it was as sincere as the last, Libra children will evaluate how fully you accept them and adjust their behavior until they know they've got it right. They only feel secure when they know they are fully loved. This makes your little Libra especially eager to enjoy your company, if not all of the time, at least as much as possible.

Those born under this sign are thinkers, but not in the strictly productive sense. Libra tries to conceive of ways to make the world more beautiful and these children see beauty not only through their eyes, but also through their feelings. A world at peace is the only one that will work for this child, who is far more sensitive than you may think. Any kind of harsh noises, hostility, or heaven forbid—a family argument—are likely to plunge this little one into a sea of tears. You must nurture these tendencies in this child but also allow for some way for your baby to understand that things can't always be perfect. You may even have to let baby cry now and then, just to teach the art of self-soothing. Provide a cuddly toy, preferably a soft stuffed animal "friend," to keep Libra company when you can't be there to hold this sweet child in your arms.

✳ YOUR LIBRA BOY ✳

Libra boys are different from the rest. They seem to know when they are dressed up to go someplace special, such as church or some family event. Your Libra boy will smile for pictures and always hope—and know—that he looks very handsome. He'll respond with broad smiles when you tell him how fashionable he looks wearing his new outfit, color-coordinated with his shiny new shoes.

While they are famous for being peaceful, Libra boys are far from being little push-overs. In some cases, the desire to assert dominance while pretending to be the "Mr. Congeniality" of the indoor play area will be evident from the start. Your son will make friends with all the other children, usually in an effort to get each one to do something for him. It is in this backhanded way that your Libra boy shows he's capable of being "the boss," while the rest of the children believe he wouldn't hurt a fly. They will rush to help him out, sensing that he really does like *everyone*. It is in this way that your Libra boy will accumulate quite an impressive collection of friends.

Yet, your Libra boy won't take well to many of the games other boys like to play. He will live very much "in his head" and might fail to see the point in roughhousing or pointlessly running up and down the field, chasing a ball. He will, instead, prefer to play strategy games and make up stories that feature him and his imaginary friends. He will be social and quite well-liked by his peers, but he won't hold all of them in esteem. Libra's devotion to what is balanced and/or beautiful will cause him to exclude those he feels are blatantly disruptive from his list of little buddies. Your Libra boy hates unfairness, and will complain bitterly about bullies being forgiven and given a second chance, particularly if one has victimized him.

Give your Libra boy the ammunition he needs to survive any kind of adverse set of circumstances. Teach him that anger is a valid emotion, and that what we do when we are angry is what really matters. Show him how to let his emotions out directly, and you'll help him to avoid many years of suffering the fate of being identified as "passive-aggressive."

✳ YOUR LIBRA GIRL ✳

Little Libra girls are definitely everything you thought you'd enjoy when you imagined the sweetness and gentleness a daughter would bring. She will love to dress up, and always ensure she looks almost perfect. From a very early age, she'll know when her headband is drooping or her diaper is showing under her skirt—and she'll want you to fix it! She will exude charm and grace, and people will comment about how beautiful she is. All of this is true, to a degree—but as her parent, you mustn't be fooled into thinking that this means that she is totally compliant and as flawless as she would like to pretend!

Your Libra girl will show much talent, especially in the arts. She'll be deeply interested in drawing and painting, dancing and singing. You might want to sign her up for dance classes or music lessons at an early age, but there are facts you need to know before you do. Famous for starting things and then never getting them finished, Libra girls must be discouraged from taking on too many different activities at one time. While it's always good to expose her to every possible avenue for her expression through the arts, it's not always possible to pay for it. Invest wisely in those things that she truly shows passion as well as talent for, and then you might see her efforts and your money bear fruit.

Before she gets too old, Libra will want to show you there's way more to her than princess outfits, tutus, and tap dancing. Libra girls have very strong minds and will be obviously intelligent from birth. It's important to be at least as enthusiastic about her academic success as you are about her artistic triumphs. She will deliberately choose friends based on their ability to keep up with her mentally, whether they seem to you like they're "fun" or not. She also needs to know that "goodness" transcends beauty, and will want to give everyone she meets a fair chance at being her friend.

Guide her to place more emphasis on the activities that will help her most in the long run by allocating your applause accordingly. Libra girls, above all else, want to be "liked," and no one (at least at this stage of her life) will be as important to impress as you.

✳ TALENTS AND AFFINITIES ✳

THE ARTS

As little Libras love to make the world "prettier," they'll have a natural talent for most of the arts, but especially writing, painting, and dance. You can begin with allowing this child's imagination to be expressed through finger paints and tap dancing on the tile floor at home; but formal training will eventually be best for your Libra, as these children are not the most self-motivated ones you'll ever meet.

LANGUAGE

Talking at an early age is one way in which your Libra will show intelligence and a desire to connect with others. There's no "right" time to start reading to a baby, but for your little Libra you'll want to begin much earlier than anyone would guess. For a non-musical lullaby, try reading lyrical prose or sonnets to this brilliant little child, and the beauty in these forms of language will make an impression that Libra will run with—maybe even, one day, to the nearest library.

STRATEGY GAMES

Something odd and paradoxical about peaceful little Libra children is their ability to absorb the rules of games and create strategies for winning. They see both sides of every situation, and although they're known for being peaceful, and supposedly detest a noisy argument, they are fiercely competitive when engaged in mental pursuits. Early introductions to board games and children's chess teams will nurture this ability.

☀ LITTLE CHALLENGES ☀

Libra doesn't seem all that hard to manage, especially as an infant and young toddler. So full of talent and potential, won't this little artistic urchin automatically become the perfect lawyer, poet, or military strategist? Probably not, especially if you don't provide Libra with adequate challenges and consistent boundaries. Like most human beings, Libra seeks out pleasure, affection, and gratification, but most of all Libra likes to find ways around doing work! When absorbed by passion for finger painting or dancing, this child can be extremely focused and excel beyond your wildest dreams. Yet when confronted with the boring basics of learning how to tie shoes or tell time, Libra will try to outwit you in desperate attempts to get around doing it and finding an "easier way." The inventor of Velcro shoe fasteners must have been a Libra! The more mundane a task is the harder Libra will find it to master. If half the energy of what it takes to find a way around doing the work were to be put into actually getting it done, many tearful fights would be avoided. Always be firm about getting Libra to "follow the leader" and make sure it's understood that the leader is *you*.

✳ DISCIPLINE ✳

It's so hard to fathom that this small, graceful being would ever do anything "wrong," but don't be fooled. If you want your Libra baby to grow up to be happy she must be able to get along with the rest of the world. Most of Libra's transgressions will involve jumping the gun; for example, displaying impatience and touching things that are simply too pretty to resist! When you go head to head with a Libra child, you'll be confounded by the way your little one seems to think of some way around your logic. The very best thing to do, when you must show your disapproval, is exclude the child from your activities. There's no doubt that the "time out" chair is the very best friend for most parents of Libra children. Your little Libra must not be allowed back into your activity until an apology and an attitude change are delivered. Be firm, but don't yell—you'll only provoke a very loud meltdown.

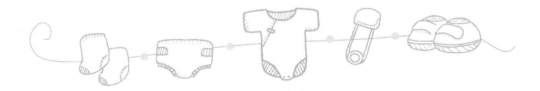

FAVORITE THINGS

SING THESE SONGS WITH YOUR LIBRA CHILD	❯ **"Supercalifragilisticexpialidocious":** For Libra, wordplay is tongue candy.	❯ **"Bicycle Built for Two":** Libra's desire to be half of a pair, in song!	❯ **"You Are So Beautiful":** Your Libra darling is certain to agree.
WATCH MOVIES LIKE THESE WITH YOUR LIBRA CHILD	❯ *Sleeping Beauty:* What Libra believes she is.	❯ *Garfield: The Movie:* This tale of a not so ambitious cat includes romance and lessons about friendship that your little Libra will love.	❯ *Cinderella:* A rags-to-riches girl meeting Prince Charming has lots of material to fuel Libra's beautiful dreams.
PLAY THESE GAMES WITH YOUR LIBRA CHILD	❯ **Patty Cake:** Libra knows you're there and likes it that way.	❯ **Dress Up:** Young Libra girls love kitten heels and lip-gloss.	❯ **Play Fighting:** Young Libra boys need a safe way to be their inner warrior.
READ THESE BOOKS, RHYMES, AND FAIRY TALES TO YOUR LIBRA CHILD	❯ **Rudyard Kipling's** *Just So Stories:* Libra simply can't hear "dearest darling" often enough.	❯ **"Jack and Jill":** Libra can't conceive of anyone going up the hill alone.	❯ *Little Snow-White:* Even boy Libra babies are down with being "the fairest one of all."
TREAT YOUR LIBRA CHILD TO THESE FOODS	❯ **Beets:** Veggies disguised as sweetness and pretty color.	❯ **Cranberry Juice:** Libra needs lots of it to keep the kidneys and bladder in tone.	❯ **Star Fruit:** Nutritious, sweet, and pretty, too!

Note: Libra isn't usually a huge eater, but will show preferences for foods that resemble the Libra personality—sweet and beautiful.

LIBRA'S BABY STYLE

Elegant, simple, yet distinctive. Libra looks best when dressed in plain colors. Avoid excessive prints, clashing colors, bows, frills, and the like.

GIRLS: She'll favor one or two accessories, but will pull anything excessive out of her hair and off her diaper.

BOYS: You'll be shocked at how early he notices the elegant lines of "designer" clothing and shows a clear preference for it.

LIBRA'S ENVIRONMENT

In terms of decorations and equipment, the less clutter the better. Keep Libra's room peaceful and calm, in one or two colors only. Add soft music at naptime if needed and keep out bright lights and noisy neighbors.

CALMING LIBRA

If your little Libra starts to cry, there's probably something wrong—at least as far as Libra is concerned! Libra avoids being unpleasant just for the effect of it. Loneliness will be Libra's number one gripe. Rarely do these gentle babies have problems with colic or general crankiness. The best way to calm Libra is to hold your baby and move around. Just make sure you do so gently and gracefully! This baby can often misinterpret being "bounced" as your way of saying you're not happy with his behavior.

Should you be unable to stay with Libra, or if you wish to teach your baby how to be "alone," remember that the most calming sound to Libra is words. Vocal music, or better yet, a book on tape, would work very well as background noise to lull Libra off to sleep.

✳ STIMULATING LIBRA ✳

Libras get bored easily, so don't fail to provide plenty of exciting activities for play time. Here are some favorite toys:

- **Building Blocks:** Let Libra learn how to achieve balance first hand.
- **Talking Books:** Libra will go crazy wondering when the "little person in there" will come out.
- **Art Supplies:** Even as an infant, Libra will want to make something "pretty."

✳ LIBRA'S LEARNING STYLE ✳

Most Librans learn by being told in words what to do. Although they can be rather visually oriented also, logic always appeals to them. Once your little Libra gets to school, it would be best to put her in an environment that is peaceful and, at least to some degree, structured. A free-for-all kind of classroom or one that is too oriented toward independent learning might not be the best thing for your lovely Libra child.

PARENTING LIBRA

If your sign is . . .

ARIES

You and Libra are at opposite ends of the spectrum, so try to remember this from the start. While you have much to offer one another, Libra will view his own position as one that is superior to yours. While your child might admire your sheer physical force and the ability to be courageous and kind at the same time, it will be hard for him to understand your lack of emphasis on the intellectual and your penchant for physical exercise. While Libra can be quite competitive, he will deliberately defy you when it comes to enjoying the same games. Give Libra the space and permission to be different from you and before you know it you'll notice how much your child actually wants to be just *like* you.

Libra won't respond well to any outbursts of temper. In fact, it's important to give this child peace and quiet from the start. Avoid holding your Libra child while you're watching noisy and/or violent TV shows or movies, and be careful when playing games that seem to be rough. Although Libra can eventually grow to be as strong and fearless as you, it's an acquired taste. Feed your little Libra small bits of action at a time.

TAURUS

You and Libra share a favorite planet, Venus, but you appreciate it in entirely different ways. Not nearly as sensual or materialistic as you are, Libra disdains overindulgence and could find your acquisitiveness to be crude. Don't let this make you believe that Libra can't spend money, though! The average Libra child always chooses the most expensive option in clothing, toys, and hobbies. You'll have to teach Libra that money is something that must be worked for. You might be driven to the brink of madness by what you view as Libra's laziness, but if you're willing you might learn something about the slow process of appreciating beauty and following your true passion.

Libra will be grateful to you for the material things that you provide, and will appreciate how easy it seems for you to stick with a job until it's finished. Keep showing the things you want Libra to learn by example, and your industrious nature is quite likely to rub off! From the early years, teach Libra that money isn't everything, but it might be the only thing that can buy many of the things Libra wants!

GEMINI

You'll feel as though you've discovered your own best buddy the first time you see your little Libra. Early to talk and easy for you to understand, this brilliant child shares the element air with you. Beware, though, of unintentionally creating a miniature adult out of your Libra child. Everybody deserves to be a baby, and Libra enjoys the feeling of being pampered and coddled far more than you ever did. Try to emphasize the physical closeness that's so precious to a small child—and essential for building your bond. Rather than slinging your baby on your back or placing your precious package in a jogger stroller, just stand still and hold this wonderful being while you make soul-to-soul contact through your eyes.

Libra will admire you and be amused by your funny jokes. The two of you will enjoy word games and goofy songs together. The one thing you need to try harder at is administering discipline. Libra, though seeming unassuming and docile, can easily walk rings around you logically, given the chance. This clever strategy will be used to pull the wool over your eyes when you least expect it, and it can manifest at a really early age! Stay on your toes, be sharp and skillful, and you'll show this baby who the cleverest of them all *really* is, without even trying.

CANCER

The Libra child's graceful manner and adorable gestures will win your heart. Your baby will appreciate all the things you do to be the (nearly) perfect parent, too. You're ultrasensitive to the way other people show affection, so be aware that Libra isn't as cuddly and kissy as you are. Direct expressions of closeness are rare, but when your beautiful child reaches up to stroke your cheek in love and admiration, you're sure to melt, and probably weep with joy.

Your domestic skills and your emotional intelligence will be the things that Libra admires about you, but don't expect this child to mirror your talents. Libra is a very dependent type, and wants you to witness every new experience, each first utterance, and of course every source of inconvenience! When something falls over or needs to be cleaned up or put away, Libra will be totally convinced you can do it *so* much better, and insist that's why you must do it. To keep your charmingly deceptive child from morphing into a helpless but ardent dictator, institute consistent and structured activities that involve picking up toys and keeping clothing clean and neat from a very early age.

LEO

You'll be proud and happy about having this Libra child. So tiny, so cute, so pleasant, and so adoring, this little one seems to be designed to make your parental fantasies come true. The part you don't know about when you first fall for your baby, though, is just how much work it will take to get this child to be anywhere near what you consider strong and self-sufficient.

Libra has a lot of trouble making decisions, and although this child seems to always be starting something new there will rarely be enough follow-up for your satisfaction. Libra needs more of your focus, so teach it by reading one story the whole way through before starting a new one. Your strong desire to bring the best out in this baby will help develop talents in the visual arts, dance, drama, and music, but you'll also want to push and encourage more self-reliance. This can be done even while little Libra is still in the crib, by insisting on naptimes and patiently waiting out a few wails while Libra learns the art of self-comforting. The more you set strong boundaries, the better prepared your Libra will be for real life.

VIRGO

You'll love to look at your nearly perfect Libra, but you'll have to learn early to forget about pressing for the small stuff with this pleasant-but-stubborn child. Libra's goal in life is to keep everything as it is, and in many instances this ends up meaning doing as little work as possible. You won't fall easily for this child's charms because you have little or no tolerance for laziness. Despite your frustrations, you'll admit you have the most amazing, talented, and adorable child on the block.

You and Libra don't always see eye-to-eye because you deal with practical things and Libra is all about appreciating beauty. Your idea of a nursery, with sanitized sheets and pure white walls, will seem too sterile to this child. Frilly and superfluous items, from lace and fringe on the bedclothes to delicately dancing figures looming over baby's crib, are essentials to your Libra child. Stimulate your baby's artistic sensibilities with exposure to the visual arts and a steady dose of background music that soothes both of your souls. You will learn almost as much as you teach with this baby, including how to stop working long enough to see and smell the roses.

LIBRA

What a thrill it is to have a beautiful little one with a sweet smile, tender eyes, and a disarming disposition—just like you! You'll smile and shake your head often as you watch this baby grow. Libra will charm you with coy smiles and offerings of love, yet you'll know what's really going on better than this child does.

Libra will try to do everything the easy way, as you well know, so the task of parenting this baby will pose certain challenges to you. Can you attest to the fact that hard work is usually the fastest way to getting what you want? You may have suffered as you learned this lesson, so teach it to your child as soon as possible. Instead of bringing everything over to little Libra while he poses in a regal position, entice him to roll, crawl, or toddle his way to it. As you well know, no Libra alive will try hard to do something unless there's a big reward at the end of the process. For your baby, this might be a favorite stuffed toy, a soothing teether, or a treat that's as beautiful as it is yummy.

SCORPIO

Your Libra child's beautiful appearance and sweet personality will embody the many reasons you want to have a baby to call your own. Libra will appreciate your protective nature, to a degree. You'll enjoy the way Libra does what's necessary to please you, and if you use your impressive set of smarts, you can use Libra's need to be loved and accepted to your advantage.

Few parents on earth are able to convey disapproval or disdain with one look the way you can. Be careful, though, because the idea of being out of your good graces could cause your little Libra to fear you at an early age. Reserve your most derisive glances for instances when you know Libra is pushing all your buttons or is in real physical danger. The rest of the time, you can let Libra know that no one will be getting much over on you by gently ignoring any unwanted behavior. While micromanaging this baby's affairs won't work well, little Libra does like to know you're there to watch, protect, and offer positive reinforcement. Encourage Libra to use that rather magnificent mind to unlock enigmas, from simple sorting boxes to pretty picture floor puzzles.

SAGITTARIUS

You'll be overjoyed to hold your Libra baby for the first time—just don't drop the package! It takes time to get used to this baby's even, yet reserved, energy. Unlike you, this baby doesn't move without substantial motivation, but one day you'll be thrilled by the fascinating conversations that you'll share. Yes, you'll be restricted to a few syllables at a time for about the first year, so you must use nonverbal cues to convey to your astoundingly cute new addition what you know is best. Make this into a little game and you'll both get big laughs.

Tiny, precious little baby Libra is definitely harmless looking enough, but from the beginning you need to know this baby has an advantage over you. Your trusting, kind, and lenient way with baby is exactly what Libra is hoping for! This little child could soon have you working around his demands unless you set boundaries. That word alone makes you flinch, but if you don't soon set regular and predictable parameters for this child, you'll be in trouble; and you won't be doing baby Libra any big favors. If you prove to be a good parent by laying down the law, however, you'll always be the best of friends.

CAPRICORN

Poor little Libra! This cute character has no idea what is to come in this rather appropriate parent-child relationship. While you certainly dote over your newborn, you also will provide ample doses of structure and insist on certain levels of behavior that head off Libra's charming way of working *around* authority at the pass.

It's important to mix love and admiration with wit and adult-type guidance. One good way to get your point across to your Libra is to make teaching "right and wrong" into a game. Reward Libra with smiles and goofy noises that are a sure-fire way to get the little gurgler giggling, and make funny sounds and sirens when you want the baby to stop doing something dangerous or annoying. Stern voices and abrupt changes in mood shake up the Libra psyche. Because Libra is so intent on keeping the peace, your baby will avoid confrontations, so you have to be very direct about what you expect from your child. Keep your sense of humor. While you'll teach Libra about the value of boundaries and a strong work ethic, this clever child will bring out your silly side, and without even knowing it, demonstrate the therapeutic power of laughter.

AQUARIUS

The teensy little toes and smooth skin on your Libra baby confirm your suspicions. Yes, you've just brought home the best child ever! Before you get too complacent, though, you should know there is going to be as much work as there is play to raising baby Libra. First of all, while this child is very bright, she needs to just "be a baby" for at least the first year. The artistic and interpersonal talents tend to blossom first, and then the fine mind will emerge. You and this child can easily be "soulmates," but first you must get Libra's attention and earn her trust.

Libra needs to know you're watching what's going on, whether this is during feedings or while you're changing her. It's not easy for you to remain focused on the mundane (and somewhat disagreeable) tasks associated with caring for a small infant, but you must. In order for this baby to feel safe and secure you have to prove that you really are "always there." As this baby grows, you will most likely become close friends, but until then you must do your best to prove you're worthy of Libra's trust and allegiance.

PISCES

This miniature human is beautiful to you in every way. You'll sense the delicacy of your little Libra's soul and will try your best to protect it from anything that would create emotional scars. You and Libra are alike in that you don't care for loud noises or disruptive behavior. The two of you can live in your own little world, and Libra will be very happy with the fantasy scenes you create in the nursery and beyond.

Still, while you're watching over this little soul you must remain very much aware of the real world. This baby will challenge you to see if you're really watching when he does something naughty or even potentially dangerous. It's especially important to develop greater focus and to show you're capable of keeping it so your Libra child will grow to have self-esteem as well as confidence in your capability to be the adult in the room. Teach Libra more about the spiritual side of life by reading stories that pertain to magic and godlike beauty; you will give your child a great gift by showing him by example that faith in a power greater than our minds is the most valuable thing we can own.

CHAPTER 8

Scorpio:

Still Waters Run Deep

BORN BETWEEN: October 22–November 21
RULING PLANET: Mars – The nighttime, strikes-like-a-ninja side
EXALTED PLANET: None needed. Scorpio's strength is so deep and profound that Mars is
the only planet that thrives in it.
COLOR: Black and Purple
GEMSTONES: Topaz, Obsidian

HE QUIET LITTLE ONE YOU'RE HOLDING, with the intense stare and quiet sense of mastery, was born under the sign of Scorpio for a reason. At this child's birthday time, the earth quiets down from the celebration of the harvest to gather energy so that it might regenerate life once again. Scorpio is a *water* sign, and it is *fixed*, which means that while your Scorpio child will be very emotionally oriented, she will also be very stubborn about seeing life any other way. This doesn't mean your child won't be intelligent—quite the contrary. It's just that this child will take you to your limits when it comes to keeping up with her emotional IQ.

Scorpio is always taking what she sees, hears, or feels, and processing it. You might not have meant anything when you used the words "You're too small," but Scorpio heard something different. Now Scorpio will struggle to show you just how "big" she is and do it with more determination than you thought was possible. At the same time, Scorpio has worked out how to get what she wants from you without asking for it overtly. This child, partly possessive and always attentive, will thrive on opportunities to outsmart you. Unless you're terribly diligent, this will happen before you even have a chance to become aware of it.

Taking care of Scorpio's physical needs isn't so hard. For the most part, this little child won't complain as long as you keep her on a very regular schedule. If there are any problems with Scorpio, they could be associated with diaper habits. This little one likes to be in control of everything and needs a lot of privacy. Keep this in mind and try as best you can to develop an "laissez faire" attitude about this part of your little Scorpio's life. Scorpio can be very willful and could possibly display moments of almost-unbelievable stubbornness while still very young. You might not always know what to do with your Scorpio, but you'll always be astonished by the way this tot can push your buttons.

YOUR SCORPIO BOY

Scorpio boys are not like the rest of the kids on the block. For starters, they tend to play very quietly. Scorpio, always in need of some sort of "secret," will be the kind of boy to keep collections of interesting objects and not tell anyone the items are there. As long as these aren't shrimp shells from last weekend's seafood dinner or dead worms, you should be in good shape; but don't be surprised to find these things sequestered away under your Scorpio's bed.

Scorpio boys, even more than their female counterparts, are fascinated by the idea of death and regeneration. Your boy will have a strange fascination for all that is gross and ghoulish, even more than you would imagine when you hear the rhyme about boys, snails, and puppy dog tails! However, your Scorpio boy will also believe that he can heal and transform himself as well as others in his world, so while he'll be attracted to entertainment that displays death and destruction he'll also have an impulse to heal. The first little boy to run to the scene of a playground mishap is usually a Scorpio, armed with innate knowledge on how to make someone feel better.

Scorpio boys are also very good at solving mysteries. Your son will love to play "spy" and generally sneak around the house. For his—and your—safety, anything that could possibly be dangerous to anyone should be kept out of your little Scorpio's reach. If you think you already have it all secured, think again—then take it up a notch! Never forget how easy it is for little Scorpio to outwit you.

Later, when he goes to school, your Scorpio boy will have an above-average ability to learn. It will be important to ensure that he is well stimulated, too. If he is held back by slow learners in his class, give him some out-of-school experiences that allow him to stretch his mind and satisfy his curiosity. Help him start a bug collection or take him to the museum to learn about how the process of evolution took place over the millennia.

YOUR SCORPIO GIRL

Scorpio girls may seem to be very quiet and shy, but they really aren't. In fact, they have more courage and tenacity than you can probably imagine. Scorpio women are among the strongest female figures there are; they start out as hearty little babies, and although they need as much coddling and love as any other child, they also are capable of surviving despite incredible odds.

Scorpio girls are interested in what people have to say but even more fascinated by what they really mean. You might want to become much more conscious about the way you say things in front of your little Scorpio girl, because she will internalize whatever is said and make it a part of her psyche. Scorpios are always looking beyond the surface for hidden meanings. Like her male counterpart, the female Scorpio is fascinated about how we die and how we can bring ourselves back to life. Your little, curious, and sometimes pushy Scorpio girl could one day grow up to be a fantastic surgeon or insightful psychotherapist because of this ability.

Your Scorpio girl will be tougher than some of the boys in her class, and the other girls may be somewhat afraid of her as a result. You'll want to monitor these situations to ensure that your child is not getting accused of being a bully. While a Scorpio rarely launches overt attacks, your daughter may plot out revenge, but only if provoked! Try to get a dialogue going between the two of you that keeps you informed not only of what kinds of things are happening with her grades, but also with her friendships. Scorpio girls rarely have tons of friends because they take so long to build trust. Once they let someone get close, though, they usually remain friends for a lifetime.

Give your Scorpio girl a little bit of time each day to be alone. Every Scorpio requires some private time and a few little secrets. Your Scorpio daughter will be the kind to keep a journal, but even then she won't write down *everything*! Scorpio always has to have some kind of secret in order to feel safe and "in control." If you're smart, you'll allow some of this so your daughter isn't tempted to treat you to a strong dose of the legendary "fire and brimstone" Scorpio temper.

TALENTS AND AFFINITIES

SCIENCE

Scorpio is always looking for answers and will be very curious about how the world works. From the names of various rocks and stones to the things that make one animal or plant different from another, your child will always be tuned into the world, viewing it as a gigantic puzzle just waiting for that one last missing piece, which will of course be supplied by . . . Scorpio!

LANGUAGE

Scorpio is sparing with words for the most part, but will be eager to learn more about how to express the feelings he has from early on. Your Scorpio child's first sentences will probably begin with the words "I feel," and you'll have to cherish these moments. As Scorpio grows older, he will grow increasingly reluctant to talk about what's going on in that dark and mysterious world of emotion.

MUSIC

Scorpio will very easily get lost in the world of music, and this can be a good thing. All of those hidden emotions need a healthy outlet, and few are better than music. Scorpio is more likely to be a violinist, cellist, or bassoonist than a guitar soloist, but you will have to watch your little Scorpio to see what instrument(s) holds the most attraction and let it go from there.

FAVORITE THINGS

SING THESE SONGS WITH YOUR SCORPIO CHILD
> **"Five Little Ducks"**: Practice for coping when Scorpio leaves the nest.

> **"My Grandfather's Clock"**: Scorpio knows—all good things come to an end.

> **"Them Bones"**: Scorpio's medical prowess leads to early studies in anatomy.

WATCH MOVIES LIKE THIS WITH YOUR SCORPIO CHILD
> *Despicable Me:* Scorpio will learn that one-upping someone else shouldn't always be a priority.

> *Monsters, Inc.:* This charming tale of overcoming scary creatures will fuel Scorpio's fearlessness.

> *Flushed Away:* Scorpio will giggle for hours over this story of coming up from the underworld.

PLAY THESE GAMES WITH YOUR SCORPIO CHILD
> **Seven Up:** A good indoor play game for Scorpio's inquiring mind.

> **Cops and Robbers:** Lets Scorpio exercise law-enforcement muscles.

> **Hide and Seek:** Scorpio's sixth sense will help hunt people down.

READ THESE BOOKS, RHYMES, AND FAIRY TALES TO YOUR SCORPIO CHILD
> *Journey to the Center of the Earth:* Scorpio enjoys digging deep and finding treasure.

> *Three Blind Mice:* A merry rhyme with a dark ending, but Scorpio will be highly entertained by recounting the tale.

> *The Ugly Duckling:* Scorpio is always happy to reveal the beauty that lies within, and will embrace this story with enthusiasm.

TREAT YOUR SCORPIO CHILD TO THESE FOODS
> **Yogurt:** Probiotics are excellent for Scorpio's iffy constitution.

> **Grape Juice:** The deep purple will attract Scorpio like a moth to your porch light.

> **Avocado:** Scorpio will like the texture—and the huge seed hiding inside.

✳ LITTLE CHALLENGES ✳

No one will tell you that raising Scorpio is the easiest thing you'll ever do. These children are very special and require your love and attention to a greater degree than you might imagine. While they can be strong and seem to be somewhat self-serving, they are actually very sensitive and will be crushed at the slightest sign you are displeased. You must earn Scorpio's respect, to be sure, and you'll never do it by kowtowing to your child. Scorpio, under most circumstances, is smart enough to know what the rules are, and when your child violates them it's more because he wants to than because of forgetfulness or impulse.

Never underestimate Scorpio's ability to hold out if you get into a staring contest, or into a standoff over a favorite toy or more time at the amusement park. You must think of Scorpio as a ninja, one who strikes fast and furiously but possibly not right out in the open. While pretending to do your will, your Scorpio child could just as easily ignore you, create an elaborate cover story, and do what he wants anyway. This might sound like a teenager's trick, but you can expect to see such shenanigans unfold at a much earlier age. For the sake of Scorpio's safety, maintain a certain degree of suspicion. The little four-year-old who says she's going off to take a nap could wander out to a street or a backyard swimming pool, so you have to be extra-sharp.

DISCIPLINE

You really can't win a face-to-face confrontation with Scorpio, because your child won't let you; nor can you use the same old punishment over and over again, because Scorpio will get used to it and the punishment's effectiveness will be diminished. If you really must punish Scorpio, you have to be pointed about it.

For example, if your little two-year-old decides to smear finger paints on your brand new car, you will have to figure out what matters most to Scorpio. Is it going to the petting zoo, or taking that trip to the science museum you promised? Perhaps she's looking forward to a visit with Grandma or a special playdate?

Scorpio likes to think things will go off as planned and can't imagine that you'd really cancel something that significant for a mere infraction of the rules. Yet, if you expect to keep this child from running your life and potentially ruining some of your precious possessions, you must assert your power without equivocation. Eliminating a favorite activity from Scorpio's plan is an excellent way to do this. Remember, your little scorpion is smart, but if you're tough he'll think again before doing something surreptitious or revengeful in return!

SCORPIO'S BABY STYLE

You might think it's odd, but your little one will like dark colors rather than the traditional pastels that come to mind when you think "baby." Yes, it would be weird to dress your child in a black diaper cover with matching black nursery cap, but if Scorpio could dress herself, that might be what she'd be wearing!

GIRLS: She might like that pinkish-purple that's so popular with little girls, but forget about the pale stuff. She'll also enjoy wearing velvet and lace—possibly together.

BOYS: He'll pick the black one every time, and will choose favorite sports teams because they wear it, too.

SCORPIO'S ENVIRONMENT

This sounds odd, as so many children try to do all they can to get your attention, but for Scorpio to be completely happy you have to provide a place for him to be alone and in private. Scorpio likes to be in quiet, dark places, so be sure to get highly functional window coverings and put a few items for Scorpio to cuddle with in there, too. This alone time is essential for Scorpio's spiritual life and creative development.

CALMING SCORPIO

Scorpio feels deeply and cries very hard. It can be alarming to hear your little one's wails, even if you know it's just mealtime or the diaper is in need of changing. Sometimes Scorpio's digestive system can go haywire, and there can also be urinary tract problems, as these are the weak parts of many Scorpio bodies. If your little one doesn't calm down within a reasonable amount of time, investigate. Scorpio will rarely cry just to draw attention. If there's still nothing wrong, assume there's an emotional bruise that needs to heal. Hold your Scorpio close until she's convinced that you love her with all your heart, and always will.

STIMULATING SCORPIO

Scorpio is the kind of child who will get involved in games and toys that are beyond his age range. Try some of these:

- **A Dollhouse or Action Sets:** Watch and listen while Scorpio creates characters and develops subplots.
- **A Punching Bag:** This is something you can leave hanging around Scorpio's "private" area for Scorpio to vent pent-up frustrations upon!
- **Musical Instruments:** Even if your Scorpio doesn't become Yo-Yo Ma, playing any instrument can be therapeutic for this little scorpion.

SCORPIO'S LEARNING STYLE

Scorpio absorbs information at alarming rates. When your Scorpio child is curious about something, there had better be plenty of sources of information because he will turn over stones—literally—in search for answers. In school, this means your child will need understanding teachers who won't look upon his requests for more sources as an annoyance. Always keep a brisk dialogue about academic questions going with your Scorpio child. If he isn't stimulated, those grades could go in the wrong direction.

PARENTING SCORPIO

If your sign is . . .

ARIES

You might think you're strong and aggressive, but you've just met your match! Your little Scorpio child, cute and sweet as she might be, is going to challenge you more than you thought possible. Your new child operates almost entirely in the realm of emotions and it's not always clear what those feelings are. You might have to struggle to figure out what's wrong when the baby is crying, and your quick motions and sudden bursts of activity will startle this young and sensitive child.

If you scramble to be the "super parent," changing the diaper faster and feeding more furiously, you'll only make matters worse. Without doubt, you'll have to compromise with your child just enough to get little Scorpio to stop feeling as though life is zipping by far too fast. When you just can't seem to connect with Scorpio, seize on what you have in common: an affinity for the rough-and-tumble nature of the rambunctious planet Mars! The two of you could giggle together to a slapstick movie or create a better bond by testing little Scorpio's strength (and play acting to let the baby "win") in a thumb war or arm-wrestling match.

TAURUS

You and your little Scorpio have more in common than you might think, but you might not notice it at first. This tiny tot will seem to be very "deep" in that she takes in everything that happens on an emotional level. Oversensitivity and a bit of whininess might manifest while your Scorpio baby is very young. It will be your job to establish an environment that feels safe and secure so baby Scorpio feels that she has landed in the right place, at least.

Later, as your Scorpio child begins to express her own personality, you might notice that the child is just as steadfast—or as some of your friends and relatives call it, "stubborn"—as you are. You might want Scorpio to eat that broccoli, but if she doesn't feel like it, there's not much likelihood of it happening! Take heart, because if any one parent has a chance of persuading Scorpio to do something that's not on the agenda it would be you! That's why it's good to remember how Scorpio needs to take things slow, doesn't love change, and needs to know what to expect next. Does that sound familiar? Of course it does, because your Scorpio baby really isn't all that different from you!

GEMINI

You might be a little bit worried about how you'll connect with your Scorpio child. Of course you'll love this child, but you might wonder how you'll be able to communicate. Scorpio is the "strong and silent" type, while you're . . . certainly not silent! This difference between you will be apparent from the outset, because your little Scorpio will not be thrilled when you talk and talk, as you tend to do.

You must learn to communicate with this child in a different way. Use eye contact, gentle touch, and other facial expressions and watch your baby respond. You have to remember that everything that makes noise sounds several levels louder by the time it reaches Scorpio's little ears. This child's sensitivity will always be a reminder to you that it isn't always best to "talk it out."

As your little one grows, you'll find that you need to establish a strong authority over your Scorpio. You can be friends, but you must also establish and retain your role as parent. If you don't, you'll soon find that little Scorpio will have you dancing at the end of a string, and that's just not the way it's supposed to be.

CANCER

Your itsy-bitsy Scorpio baby will seem to be even more adorable than you hoped. This child is just as sensitive as you are, if not more so. This makes it easy for the two of you to relate, but you still must be very careful. While Scorpio is a lot like you, there is more to this baby than what meets the eye.

Scorpio has a very deep and secretive aspect to his personality, and because you're very vulnerable you need to be aware of it. This is not the kind of child who will willingly tell you everything. You're going to have to use your own intuition to pick up on what's going on, from the times when your little Scorpio is crying because there's a slight ear infection to the moment years later when your child comes home from high school, upset over the refusal of a prom invitation. Scorpio wants you to guess at what's wrong, but he wants you to be wrong! This can be confusing to you, and at times your feelings might get hurt.

As much as you'd like to be the one who gets closest to Scorpio, you might not always receive that privilege. Your Scorpio child needs you to keep a safe, parental distance so you can remain a reliable and safe authority figure, rather than just another "best friend."

LEO

Your Scorpio will take to you right away because she knows how to charm you. That's right. If you believe this little baby is anything but as bright as you are, you're in trouble. While it will be wonderful to drink in the admiration emanating from your young child's eyes, you must be careful not to delude yourself into thinking this baby is going to be easy to parent.

You have an easy time understanding most of your child's temperament, because you are both very determined people. The stubbornness you see in your Scorpio, however, is somewhat more difficult to turn around than your own immovable tendencies.

Scorpio is looking for excellence in everything, and unless she finds some in you there could be difficulties. For the most part, living with this little scorpion will be pleasant but it will also be challenging. You'll be tested over and over again as your child attempts to see if you're as worthy of respect as you purport to be. Of course, your integrity, honesty, and ambition will more than meet Scorpio's expectations, and your baby will come to rely on you to help train him to become a fine and successful citizen.

VIRGO

The Scorpio baby is very sweet and quiet, and you'll like the way she responds to your efforts to get her on a schedule. Indeed, Scorpio likes to have regular rhythms and predictable patterns in her life. Also, the two of you are on similar missions—to find excellence and/or perfection. That's why it's going to be fun to raise this child, especially after she gets past the high-intensity caretaking stages.

You and Scorpio may not always agree on what's interesting, though! While you're focused on hygiene and cleanliness, this deeply emotional and curious child will touch just about anything if it means she'll find out what it is and what it's supposed to do. You might be horrified when your Scorpio toddles over to you with a dead bird or goldfish in her tiny hand! Although you will be appalled, it's best not to show it. Sometimes Scorpio will do these things just for the shock value, and if you allow this kind of thing to send you off balance you'll find it difficult to maintain the proper parent-child relationship that's so essential to this child's well-being.

LIBRA

Your little Scorpio will be a treasure to you and although you might not always think so, the two of you probably have a lot in common. Scorpio is a little bit less concerned about what's "pretty," but the two of you share a deep curiosity and the need for a lot of intellectual stimulation.

This child will provide you with plenty to challenge your mind, but the problem might be that no matter how hard you try to think things through the answers might not come from your brain. Scorpio is deeply emotional and needs you to meet him on that level at some point in your relationship.

Scorpio's emotional nature will be an enigma to you at times, but it's best to just let it be that way. Your child needs you to be strong and unwavering in your logic if he is to learn how to survive childhood. Your sense of fairness and your ability to see both sides of any situation will help Scorpio come out of his rather one-sided view of things. Talk about what's "fair," but try as much as possible to let Scorpio know you're on his side. That's essential.

SCORPIO

Your relatives and friends will be highly amused when they hear you have a Scorpio child! Little do they know how happy you are, though! At last, there's someone in the household who's as capable as you are at seeking out ways to be the best at as many things as possible. It's going to be interesting to see what unfolds as you raise this baby over the years, and if you've ever seen what happens when two scorpions fight over the same space, you have some idea why!

Your Scorpio child will sense you picking up on her emotional signals, and you have to be stable and sure about your own emotional state, because she will read yours. There will be games where you both wait to see who blinks first, and you'd better bring eye-wetting drops!

You know you can "manage" your little scorpion by doing all the right things—maintaining a regular schedule, establishing firm boundaries and administering emotional nourishing that really comes from your heart. By doing this, you'll show your child it really is possible to share your heart without getting it stomped on. There's no greater gift you can present to your brilliant, perceptive, and charming "mini-me."

SAGITTARIUS

You and your little Scorpio will have a very interesting interchange. If you take one look at this infant, you'll realize that she isn't very much like you at all. Where this child seems to be guarded and afraid, you're wide open and wear your heart right on your sleeve.

Both of you are intellectual giants, but you have different ways of gathering your knowledge. While you are always ready to spread your wings to go exploring, Scorpio will look in every possible nook and cranny for answers, and they do often prove to be close to home. Although you and your Scorpio won't be swapping skills when you first meet, you will learn almost as much from being with this child as Scorpio will learn from having you as her parent.

Scorpio's moods could become a problem for you at times. Your child won't understand why you're so happy most of the time, and it will take time before she comes to appreciate the idea of seeing the world as a bright, sunny, and hopeful place the way you do. Keep giving your Scorpio child that message and she'll be sure to thank you one day.

CAPRICORN

Your little Scorpio seems exceptionally quiet and unassuming, but because you can read people so well, you already know what this child might try to do in order to get his way with you. Over time, you'll develop a very loving and mutually respectful parent-child connection, but at first it may be tough going—more for your little one than for you, though.

Scorpio is a tough one and will try with all his might to usurp your authority. In your calm, unaffected, and yet very firm way, you'll give this child exactly what he needs most—a strong and unwavering source of guidance plus a set of rules that makes little Scorpio keep jumping higher and higher to achieve his goal—to be on the receiving end of your love and approval.

At first, Scorpio will be very frustrated and it's fine to back up a bit as he learns to walk so the toddler will try harder. At some point, though, you have to let Scorpio reach the goal, and when you do this child will know you have been one of the most powerful and loving teachers he could ever ask for.

AQUARIUS

Your Scorpio child will feel like a very solid little figure as you hold the bundle of love in your arms. You'll have a feeling of pride, of course, but there might also be a slight bit of nervousness. There's something very unnerving about the way a little Scorpio baby can look at you. A sea of emotions seems to tumble behind those eyes, and for you, the idea of dealing with feelings can seem remote . . . and a little bit intimidating.

As you get used to caring for this little one, you won't be able to help yourself as you feel yourself become further detached from your purely mental and preferred state of being to meet up in the middle with your Scorpio, who will do all she can to blaze a path straight into your heart.

While Scorpio teaches you to open up emotionally, you'll have to show your child the value of thinking beyond the things that she wants. The Scorpio child can become self-centered, but with your guidance, *your* Scorpio baby will grow up to be someone who, very much like you, is dedicated to making a difference in the world.

PISCES

You and the Scorpio child have a language all your own. You'll both just know how the other is feeling, and that's why it's so crucial for you to remain on an even keel for as much of the time as possible. While your little Scorpio appreciates your sentimental and almost psychic affinity, there is also a need for Scorpio to have a strong, stable environment. Without that, your child will have a harder time establishing firm footing.

You must also find ways to command more than Scorpio's love; you must earn his respect. This won't be all that easy of course, but it can be done! You'll have to build up boundaries that you don't always like to create, but in this case you must. Take time for yourself, and come each and every time Scorpio cries for you. You'll know by the nature of the noises your baby makes if it's something urgent or not. Keep up your connection with your center through meditation and/or prayer, and as much as you want to let Scorpio walk all over you, create those boundaries and stick to them. This is the best form of love you can really give to your little scorpion.

CHAPTER 9

Sagittarius:

Your Bundle of Sunshine

BORN BETWEEN: November 22–December 20
RULING PLANET: Jupiter – The bright and sunny daytime side
EXALTED PLANET: None needed! Jupiter's huge "personality" fills all of Sagittarius's needs.
COLOR: Royal Blue and Turquoise
GEMSTONES: Turquoise and Chrysocolla

OUR SAGITTARIUS CAME INTO THE WORLD at the same time as the winter holidays. Could that be why this child is so pleasant so much of the time? Sagittarius is a *fire* sign, but it's a highly refined form of fire—kind of like electricity. It is also a *mutable* sign, which allows your little Sagittarius to move from place to place without much bother. In fact, only one thing most Sagittarius babies *don't* like is sitting still!

You're likely to notice this right away, because the Sagittarius baby will kick and wave those little arms around just to get all that energy out of his system. Your child's personality is so sweet—much like a little puppy that doesn't really know how it's supposed to act, so it just acts on an impulse that mostly consists of love and affection. Your little one won't be entirely graceful, though, and will often have outbursts of pure exuberance and joy at the strangest times—and sometimes in some rather embarrassing places.

Don't let your Sagittarius's impishness belie the fact that your baby is as smart as they come. Your Sagittarius child is even more enthused about acquiring knowledge than he is about running around. In fact, by the time your child has completely grown, little Sagittarius will show signs of a desire to travel to any faraway place necessary, as long as there is new information at the other end of the trip.

Sagittarius children are explorers. Because of this, you're going to have to do the baby-proofing thing a few months before you thought you would have to. Because of Sagittarius's intense mental activity, it's hard for this child to remember that he is contained within a body. That's why stairways must be blocked off and electric sockets securely plugged up around this incredible, joyful, and brilliant little live wire.

✳ YOUR SAGITTARIUS BOY ✳

The Sagittarius boy will exhibit all of the aggressive and physically robust traits you would expect and an early exposure to sports of some kind is advisable. This little one will take any excuse to run like the lightning—and could be very talented at games such as soccer or football. Sagittarius boys are also in need of targeting games that might include archery, trap shooting, and even golf.

You might get a few calls from your child's caregivers about little accidents that happen around the house or in the classroom. Sagittarius boys need a lot of time to run and release their energy; if they don't get this, their attention can drift off and they become careless. Always make sure your Sagittarius boy has adequate time to move around every day.

The Sagittarius boy loves adventure and will embrace the kinds of play that involve superheroes, pirates, and explorers. While more well-intentioned than some other boys, your Sagittarius will have an attraction to entertainment that's based on action and maybe even violence. The good news is that he's always rooting for the hero. He has a strong sense of justice, and when he sees that the right thing isn't being done, he gets very defensive. Don't worry—this ability to advocate could mean your Sagittarius boy will be a lawyer, a judge, or a politician one day. As a child, though, he might need instruction about knowing when it's a good time to stay out of the way and mind his own business.

Your Sagittarius boy will be very fascinated with all the cultures of the world and will study them at every opportunity. You might find out more than you wanted to know about the habits of certain peoples, or traditions of some obscure tribe from the other end of the world. Embracing knowledge and integrating it to bring justice to the world is the essence of your Sagittarius son's personality. Start saving up at birth because the college bills for this one are likely to be quite formidable. Fortunately, your Sagittarius son's physical prowess is the kind of thing that could earn him sports scholarships!

✳ YOUR SAGITTARIUS GIRL ✳

Sagittarius girls are strong, kind, loving, and sweet. As babies, your Sagittarius girl will be the sunshine of your life! Even if you're having a bad day, your little Sagittarius will greet you with a smile when she wakes up every morning and hug you until you think you can no longer breathe every night.

While slightly less wild and unmanageable than boys of the Sagittarius persuasion, your daughter will require a lot of physical activity. Although you may have dreams of raising a prima ballerina, it's more likely that your child will excel at basketball or hockey. This doesn't mean she can't be feminine; but you should know that your Sagittarius girl is built more for gross large motor skill–dependent activities than movement that requires grace or agility. Because people born under the sign of Sagittarius tend to have the strong thighs of the Centaur, your daughter will have powerful—and most likely long—legs. She'll be an excellent runner, so if you find yourself out of shape the first time you take her to a playground you'll want to start doing the conditioning it takes to keep up with her!

In school, your little girl will shine. She'll be interested in all her subjects and compliant with teachers' wishes, because she'll know that good behavior will be the best way for her to gain more knowledge.

Your Sagittarius girl will likely eschew activities such as playing with dolls and holding tea parties for the opportunity to run races with the boys—and probably beat them. Her innocence can be endearing, but keep her informed about the facts of life. She might find herself in a situation that rapidly runs out of her control when she first begins to encounter boys, even at a very tender age. Knowledge is power—and she'll keep telling you that. Make sure she has the information she needs, even if you think she's way too young.

Once she knows where she fits into a situation, your Sagittarius daughter will run with it, figuratively as well as literally. Her quick mind and huge heart could lead her to become a childhood advocate, a college professor, law enforcement officer, or lawyer. All you have to do is encourage her to learn!

TALENTS AND AFFINITIES

RUNNING

Little Sagittarius's powerful legs will eventually serve to help your child run like lightning! Giving Sagittarius practice, and even training, in running can be a great idea. Not only will your child learn how to run the "right" way, this extra practice could soon have him on the road to becoming a dazzling track or cross-country star!

LANGUAGE

Sagittarius likes to have fun, so when you teach your baby some first words make a game out of the process. Your child's sense of humor will easily get wrapped around words that sound funny, and the two of you will have a blast as baby Sagittarius tries to imitate you. Sagittarius will be curious about the things around your house and will ask you what they're called. Save lots of time to prepare the answers!

COMEDY

Sagittarius has a legendary sense of humor, and will make you laugh without even trying. This child will have a sense of "timing" even as a small tot and her considerable intelligence will require you to be on the ball at all times. This child will "get" and make jokes that would go over many other people's heads. Be judicious in your choice of language, for it will be repeated!

LITTLE CHALLENGES

Sagittarius is a joy to live with for the most part. If there's anything that is irritating about your little funny, happy child, it could be the way she flings most of what she owns all over the place. You might try to introduce your child to systematic ways of organizing possessions, but it won't work very well. Sagittarius's mind moves way faster than her body, and to the average Sagittarius child that pile of junk in the middle of the room *is* a filing system—of sorts! How can a child be expected to bother with putting things in their places when there are so many adventures going on all at one time?

Is there a possible way for your baby to take the "childproof" sippy cup and dump it on the carpet? You might think not—but Sagittarius will find it, completely by accident. Your child will even trip over clothing strewn in the wrong places and seem to forget there is such a thing as a clothes hamper in that room.

All this might not sound too difficult until you have to live with it. When you discover hundreds of dollars' worth of semi-delicate sports equipment or electronics sitting in the middle of the bathroom floor, you could become quite alarmed. It's important to try not to lose your temper, though. Sagittarius rarely gets angry but will fight back fiercely if challenged in this way.

DISCIPLINE

To keep Sagittarius in line, you have to teach him what is acceptable and what just isn't going to work. But you're going to have to do this by bringing out your wild child's most refined attributes without totally killing the animal instincts that are so important to his spirit.

Sagittarius is very smart, so there's no reason why this child can't learn about being more careful through the practice of reasonable consequences. If your little Sagittarius runs too far away from you, you must then restrict the area in which the baby can be left to wander freely. If Sagittarius treats the bedroom floor as though it's a trash can that you'll eventually empty on your child's behalf, remove the items that were thrown there and encourage Sagittarius to get them back, either by performing errands (garbage duty would be perfect) or paying you from an allowance. It's a process. You will teach, and Sagittarius will learn—one day.

FAVORITE THINGS

SING THESE SONGS WITH YOUR SAGITTARIUS CHILD	❯ **"East Side, West Side":** Traveling around a city brimming with activity.	❯ **"Home on the Range":** Ode to the open air.	❯ **"Up, Up and Away":** How Sagittarius gets to all those fabulous places!
WATCH MOVIES LIKE THIS WITH YOUR SAGITTARIUS CHILD	❯ *Finding Nemo:* A nice lesson about adventure for Sagittarius; with a subliminal message about being overprotective, for you!	❯ *Madagascar:* This story about animals yearning to roam free will appeal to Sagittarius.	❯ *Up:* Your little centaur will love a visual adventure that touches most of the world and many emotions as well.
PLAY THESE GAMES WITH YOUR SAGITTARIUS CHILD	❯ **Dodge Ball:** Sagittarius has no problem being agile enough to get out of the way.	❯ **Kickball:** Gets that little Sagittarius running.	❯ **Pin the Tail on the Donkey:** Tagging a tail on an animal appeals to your child's inner beast.
READ THESE BOOKS, RHYMES, AND FAIRY TALES TO YOUR SAGITTARIUS CHILD	❯ *Where the Wild Things Are:* This one will enchant Sagittarius into her thirties, maybe longer.	❯ **"Three Children Sliding":** Sagittarius will always rethink what is "possible."	❯ **"Hansel and Gretel":** Teaches Sagittarius to leave a trail and to find the way home.
TREAT YOUR SAGITTARIUS CHILD TO THESE FOODS	❯ **Turkey:** Sagittarius will love the strong, gamey taste.	❯ **Pomegranate Juice:** Rich and juicy. Mmmmmm.	❯ **Tomato Sauce:** Sagittarius loves ethnic, spicy foods.

SAGITTARIUS'S BABY STYLE

Always dress Sagittarius in something washable. This child never anticipates the kind of mess that can be made, so he just makes it anyway. It's not a deliberate thing, by the way—just make sure the clothing you choose can take a good beating and many washings!

GIRLS: Sagittarius girls will have a funky sense of style. Although they're not ultra-feminine, Sagittarius girls will mix sporty pieces with dresses and skirts. Your little girl will love wearing athletic shoes . . . everywhere!

BOYS: If you can find indestructible clothing, get some for your Sagittarius boy. Pants with double knees and stain-proof shirts are not too extreme. He'll like bright colors and enjoy wearing khaki colored pants and those multipocketed vests that are perfect for adventure.

SAGITTARIUS'S ENVIRONMENT

Impervious to noise and certainly unaware of clutter, little Sagittarius will accept what is given with gratitude and a big smile. Sagittarius lives on a big scale, so place a large beanbag or another piece of furniture your child can lounge on in between sprints up and down the hallways!

CALMING SAGITTARIUS

Sagittarius babies smile more than most, but they do have moments of discomfort and like all children, they will cry. Funny enough, the one thing that calms Sagittarius is more activity. As an infant, you might find that your sleepless baby drifts off while you're playfully moving her arms and legs or when you take her for a stroller or car ride. Later you can calm down your little archer just by changing the subject. If your child is upset because the restaurant doesn't have chicken fingers, introduce the tasty alternative of zucchini sticks dipped in "pizza sauce." Trying something new will distract Sagittarius from just about anything!

STIMULATING SAGITTARIUS

You might not think stimulation is something a child like Sagittarius needs, but in truth the more you offer your Sagittarius baby the happier he will be. Try some of these toys:

- **Toy Horns:** Sagittarius will enjoy making noise . . . *really* enjoy it. You might want to leave the room while your Sagittarius baby is playing loudly, in hopes of getting those saints to march in.
- **Balls:** From baby's first plush ball to a real soccer ball or baseball, your Sagittarius will be fascinated with the concept of throwing, catching, and running after the ball.
- **Target Toys:** Try beanbag throwing at first, but always make sure Sagittarius has games that hone that targeting skill. Darts, archery, and trap shooting can come when they are more age-appropriate.

SAGITTARIUS'S LEARNING STYLE

A voracious learner, your Sagittarius child will devour any and all kinds of information that comes her way. In school, though, Sagittarius may not always be the teacher's favorite. This won't be because of misbehavior, but more due to the endless questions Sagittarius will ask. Provide lots of outside learning adventures for your academically curious tot and you'll keep her brain stimulated in healthy ways.

PARENTING SAGITTARIUS

If your sign is . . .

ARIES

You and Sagittarius are a great parent-baby pair! You are both quite active and lively so it will be easy to give your Sagittarius child all the much-needed activity and stimulation he could possibly desire. Yet you'll need to make sure you don't ignore the intellectual side of your baby's development. While you may not be interested in the nesting habits of the birds in the Arctic, your Sagittarius certainly could be.

Be careful not to make little Sagittarius into your new best friend though. Although the two of you will have a blast doing things together—especially if they take place in the outdoors—you must let your little archer blaze his own trail. Your little one requires a lot of independence in a different way than you do. While you're looking for ways to conquer territory, Sagittarius is just out there looking around to see what it's like.

Give your child the courage and confidence to explore and enjoy what life has to offer, but, within reason, don't dictate where Sagittarius should go or what he should do upon arrival. Leave yourself open to what your child will discover without your supervision and your little Sagittarius will lead you on a few adventures, too.

TAURUS

The joyful, active little baby you hold in your arms will be more than just "a handful" for you. Sagittarius will see the world much differently than you do. Where you prefer to stay with what you have so you can protect it, Sagittarius wants to go out and see what the big wide world has to offer. This will mean you have to comfort and direct your child without dictating what she will be doing each and every minute.

Yet, you'll have to watch out for this overly active archer! There's no question that Sagittarius's abundance of curiosity can get her into a lot of trouble, so don't be lax about babyproofing the house and make sure you don't skimp on sports equipment when your little Sagittarius starts to get involved in competitive games. You might think and hope your child won't get hurt, but there's no reason to take chances. You might, in fact, constantly underestimate the energy levels this child has because you can't imagine how it's possible!

Even with all of that, you'll still enjoy raising your Sagittarius child and take great pride in all of her achievements, whether you're beaming at a school awards program or at the big game, persistently cheering from the sidelines.

GEMINI

You and your Sagittarius child might not seem to have a lot in common, but you do. In fact, the essence of your nature—the need to be free—is as important to this child as it is to you. This can be a very good thing, because you'll understand that you can't be there for every little experience your child will go through. Also, your Sagittarius isn't likely to be clingy or whiny when you have to leave her with a caretaker or at school.

On the negative side, though, you might not always feel like your child wants to be close to you or listen to your observations and musings. Although Sagittarius will be interested in you, what's more important to your child is what's happening on the other side of the world. For this child, far-flung cultures are far more fascinating than neighborhood gossip. Still, the two of you will be very good together, especially if you learn to accept and even participate in Sagittarius's physical activities. You have much to teach your little archer, and she will listen far more intently if you make a point of listening to her questions and answering them thoroughly and honestly.

CANCER

This active little baby you have squirming in your arms will test your formidable parenting skills, but you're up to the challenge! Sagittarius is quite a different type of person, and will constantly test the boundaries to make sure they are still in effect. This child is teeming with intense energy and wants to use it to make new discoveries on an almost-constant basis. While you'll be more than happy to nurture your baby through this process, you'll also need to teach Sagittarius how to remain calm and behave in ways that are socially acceptable.

You'll want to help Sagittarius develop the ability to focus and listen, so tell or read stories about adventures and battles in far-off lands. Support Sagittarius's need for extensive physical activity, too. Even if you can't keep up with this little speedster, you can surely find some safe places to allow your archer to run around. Even in Sagittarius's infancy you can provide some physical outlets for that intense energy! A parent-baby exercise class would be a good start and could be healthy for you, too. Although your Sagittarius baby won't love being coddled and contained, she'll still want to know that when the skinned knees and twisted ankles come, you'll be there to kiss them, care for them, and make them all better.

LEO

You're going to love just about every minute you spend raising your little Sagittarius! This lively little child will bring you a lot of laughs, and the two of you will thoroughly enjoy making jokes and giggling together for hours. Most of the time, Sagittarius will defer to you and behave the way you would expect; there's that air of authority about you that Sagittarius will innately respect and the fact that you're almost as enthusiastic about life as your child is will create a nice bond from the very beginning.

You will still have to do the heavy lifting when it comes to providing a disciplined life for this little explorer. Beyond babyproofing, you're going to have to teach Sagittarius that she has responsibilities to her family, friends, and community and can't always focus on having a good time. Your ability to bring out the best in your child will allow her to grow into a fun, intelligent, and responsible adult.

You'll be very proud of your Sagittarius child and she will be eternally grateful to you for making sure all that energy didn't get squandered on frivolity and folly!

VIRGO

A little bundle of liveliness, your Sagittarius will fascinate you from the beginning. You'll marvel at your child's seemingly endless supply of energy, but you could easily become puzzled at how or why he doesn't seem to know where to direct it. Of course, you can help here, and your little archer will be glad, eventually, to have had you as a parent. Your organization ability and your desire to be of use will rub off despite Sagittarius's attempts to buck your efforts.

When push comes to shove, Sagittarius is a lot like you in that he loves to please other people. While this may not manifest right away as doing chores around the house—particularly if these chores involve picking things up and putting them in their places—there will be other ways your Sagittarius will try to become endeared to you. Try not to condemn your little one for being sloppy or careless. Instead, teach Sagittarius to slow down and be more orderly, and allow Sagittarius to inspire you to become less rigid about your own habits. That way, the two of you will each learn something about spending this amazing period of time together.

LIBRA

That little archer in your arms will hold the key to your heart from the moment you first lay eyes on one another. Sagittarius children smile so broadly it's hard to imagine them ever being anything but happy and supportive. Still, you'll need to tend to your Sagittarius's needs, including a great deal of chasing after her from the time she begins to roll over, crawl, and toddle around. Your little archer will be easy to understand from the mental point of view, but your habits when it comes to physical activity will differ. While you need a lot of motivation to get up and active, Sagittarius can't stand to sit still.

This will be tiring for you, especially while your child is small. Little Sagittarius will need a lot of interesting things to do and will ask you to be the featured entertainment—

even before she is able to speak. While you'll enjoy reading "meaty" childhood stories to your child and will relate very well to her mental agility, it might not be possible to do everything your Sagittarius wants. This is when you can gently, yet firmly, teach your little archer about boundaries and demonstrate what it means to have certain limits.

SCORPIO

Holding your little Sagittarius will make you feel happy in a whole new way. This child has a sense of hope and optimism that will cheer you up no matter how depressing the news of the day might be. Still, your Sagittarius will need to learn some of life's most difficult lessons, particularly those that involve the sad truth that she won't always have reasons to be joyous.

Your emotional sensitivity will be a great asset as your Sagittarius child grows older. Even if it doesn't seem like she relates to you in this way, you'll always know when your child needs extra attention, support, or just a hug. Although not very emotionally oriented, Sagittarius is extremely affectionate. This little tyke will crawl right up into your face like a little puppy dog, and just when you think you're about to get licked, will begin to tickle you until the two of you laugh.

Create some obstacles and hurdles for your Sagittarius child to overcome because she will need to exercise the brain as much as the body in order to live up to her full potential. As usual, you'll use your emotional IQ and will know exactly what to do.

SAGITTARIUS

Congratulations on having a child with the same sun sign as you! With luck, your spouse and the rest of your relatives will be able to laugh along as you and your Sagittarius move along the road to discovery, wonder, and happiness that the two of you travel so willingly. Your enthusiasm for life will be picked up and shared by this child, so be careful! At times, it might be hard to calm your little one down.

As you well know, when you can't relax it's probably because you're not tired enough, so when you see the same thing in your little one just take her out or play a game that uses up her energy.

You'll also have to avoid always acting on your own impulses and impress upon baby Sagittarius that it's important to be structured and disciplined in life. While you and your little Sagittarius might want to play all the time, you're going to have to stop once in a while to demonstrate the importance of discipline and hard work. If you do this, your child will have what it takes to be a complete success in life.

CAPRICORN

You'll enjoy taking care of your little Sagittarius from the moment you first hold him in your arms. There's something about this spirited little one that gets you excited—not just because he is so full of enthusiasm but also because you know you're going to have to rise to a very interesting challenge. Your child will move around a lot, and sometimes run toward the path of danger without having the slightest clue. Act as a teacher, a manager, and a loving parent and show him how to behave.

Because he doesn't necessarily think about the long-term consequences of certain actions, your little one will find a little bit of trouble. That's when you can come in and (without condemning the little one) point out why it would be better if baby Sagittarius were more careful. Give your Sagittarius more leeway than you think you probably should, and let your child learn, to some degree, by example. Your consistency and emotional detachment will be useful and supportive to Sagittarius's development, but you should also let your child show his affection toward you, too. You'll definitely earn Sagittarius's respect in the long run, and your little archer will want to show you how much you're appreciated and loved.

AQUARIUS

You and your little Sagittarius will hit it off right away. This child has a basic, innocent faith in life and seems to always be smiling and laughing. In fact, Sagittarius children might be the only ones who wake up from afternoon naps cooing rather than crying, and you'll love that about your little one. You'll also adore the fact that your child shares with you a concern for the rest of the world. But while your desire to know more about other people is more political and social, Sagittarius's fascination with other cultures is more just for the sake of knowing and understanding.

Intellectual discipline is a great gift, and you can pass yours on to your Sagittarius from the beginning. Don't let your baby move from one toy or story or extracurricular activity to the next without aim or purpose. Show Sagittarius the consequences of his actions, from running off and away from you to leaving toys and shoes in the path of other people who are walking through your house. This little archer has a social awareness, but you can refine this and make it more like your global consciousness. Your child, once he is fully grown, will be eternally grateful to you.

PISCES

Your Sagittarius will be a bundle of happiness from the beginning. The two of you share a true passion for life, and although Sagittarius is far more physical and intellectual about it, there are possibilities for opening her consciousness to your more spiritual way of viewing the universe. Teach your little Sagittarius from the time she is young that there is a purpose for her life. Whether she takes to religion or spirituality or not, you will at least be giving your little archer a goal to work toward, and this is all she really needs.

You might need help, perhaps from your partner, to bring structure and discipline into your relationship with baby Sagittarius. Although both you and your child could adapt to just about any set of circumstances, it's important for your Sagittarius child to learn how to mesh with the rest of society. Because your little one will want to understand the rules and morality that govern society, she must learn about obeying them from the start. Focus more on what you can do to help this process and your Sagittarius will be off to an excellent start in life!

CHAPTER 10

Capricorn:

The Executive Baby

BORN BETWEEN: December 21–January 20
RULING PLANET: Saturn: The structured but less obsessive side
EXALTED PLANET: Mars – Because Mars loves to work!
COLOR: Slate Gray, Charcoal
GEMSTONES: Garnet, Smoky Quartz

YOUR QUIET AND QUITE SERIOUS-LOOKING INFANT was born at the time of the earth's greatest potential. Winter, although it is dark and dreary, is also the time when we are the most productive and practical because we must work our lives around the severity of the weather. Capricorn is an *earth* sign, and it is *cardinal,* which means that your Capricorn baby will be down-to-earth, but also very ambitious. Represented by the sea-goat—a strong and steady traveler capable of mastering mountains as well as the sea, Capricorn can go from the lowliest to the highest and back down again. Understanding the entire bell curve of the human potential makes Capricorn an excellent manager or executive.

You'll notice right away how your Capricorn child seems to know how to do things that are far past his age-related expectations. Try not to mistake his sense of mastery for arrogance or condescension. As it turns out, your Capricorn simply cannot wait to be an adult, so cooing and cradling will have a very limited place in your caretaking of this child.

Capricorn children are builders. They want to manifest their ideas and desires as tangible assets and really have little time for "play." Most of what they do will be more work-oriented, as they seem to be on a mission to develop the skills necessary to get out into the world! Still, there will be a side to your Capricorn that is very playful. Cultivate this by appealing to your child's wry sense of humor. Let him in on little jokes and observations you have. Although it's never appropriate to treat your child like an adult, little Capricorn will seem like one. Try to respect the way your child sees himself and don't impose infantile activities or clothing on your Capricorn baby.

✳ YOUR CAPRICORN BOY ✳

The Capricorn boy will be tough, but not in the most overt ways. While he'll be physically strong, he usually won't choose to assert himself in that way. Capricorn can have a funny way of interacting with his peers, where he just sits back and watches them without really joining in on what they're doing unless he sees the practical use of it. When the rest of the boys have made a fort that falls apart, he'll have one that he put together all on his own, still standing. Most likely, he'll probably be securely sequestered behind it, throwing a battery of snowballs at his rivals.

Capricorn is an excellent leader, and his fellows will recognize this rather early. Your son will see the utility in each individual, and in that spirit of bringing together the highest and the lowest will relate to the strongest and the weakest in the group with the same amount of respect for each of their abilities and their purposes in life.

At home, and especially during infancy, Capricorn will look to you for some comfort. Although you might go right away to some of the physical ways to show affection, Capricorn won't be particularly cuddly. You mustn't take this as an affront. Give your baby some space, and show your love by helping your infant to learn, step by step, the skills he needs to get along in the world.

More than anything you must earn Capricorn's respect. You can be silly from time to time, but your Capricorn boy will want to know he can rely on you for a steady, sane, and rational sounding board and a safe port in stormy times.

Your Capricorn boy will, in some way, be in charge of providing an executive's view of the world, and this will manifest in his work as well as in the way he takes to being educated. He needs strong, authoritative figures in his academic environment and won't do well under experimental teaching methods. Your Capricorn boy will want to take on responsibilities at an early age, too. Give him chores and reward him with an allowance. Don't hand him money for no good reason. Always allow him to stretch his abilities and reach for more and more, for that is the way he'll grow to be the strong executive he wants to be.

✳ YOUR CAPRICORN GIRL ✳

Capricorn girls can seem to be far less frivolous than most little girls. When you think she'll be thrilled to hear the story of how the princess got her man, your little Capricorn will roll her eyes. Don't let this serious and down-to-earth part of her personality lead you to believe that there's something wrong with your Capricorn girl; she is just practical to a fault and won't really buy into the whole fantasy part of childhood.

It may seem as though your Capricorn girl is a grown woman trapped in a child's body; from the time she is very small, she'll seem far more serious than other children and won't really want to play silly games. Her sense of humor will be dry and wry, as well as incredibly quick! Your Capricorn girl will be smarter than the average child, and will ask you questions and expect straight answers.

She'll need to have some purposeful chores to do around the house and she'll be attracted to activities such as Girl Scouts or maybe music lessons. If she dances, she'll be very serious about it. Let her choose what she wants to do, but try to offer serious and community-oriented activities as well as opportunities to develop her creative side.

Capricorn girls will rise to the top of the organizations they join and you'll notice this from a very early point in your daughter's life. Others in her age group recognize her executive ability and rely upon her to provide them with a more big-picture view of what they should be doing. She's going to be self-driven for the most part in school, but will need strong and respectable authority figures if you expect her to thrive. The secret to raising your Capricorn girl, in part, is in giving her walls and other obstacles to scale. Like the sea-goat that embodies her zodiac sign, your Capricorn girl will strive to reach the heights while maintaining her connection with her roots, and most especially, the love and support of her family.

✳ TALENTS AND AFFINITIES ✳

BUILDING

Capricorn children are very keen to see their ideas take concrete form. Even if you don't provide building blocks or interlocking bricks to give them materials to build with, they'll use common household objects to construct structures that satisfy the whims of their inner vision. If you treasure pots, pans, dishes, and shoes, you'll run out to buy those building toys!

LANGUAGE

Due to Capricorn's desire to be "adult" long before growing up, your little Capricorn will try to talk from the earliest moments. Don't expect the usual babbling or bubble-blowing to take place as your little Capricorn discovers speech. This child will try to imitate you and will struggle valiantly to unlock the codes that lead to speaking, reading, and writing.

BUSINESS

Never underestimate Capricorn's interest in, or ability to excel at, business! Even as a small child, your little goat will come up with ways of providing goods and services. It's okay to allow your Capricorn to have a lemonade stand or to sell old stuffed toys, but stop short of bankrolling that software company until she finishes high school.

✳ LITTLE CHALLENGES ✳

Capricorn is comparatively easygoing, but as with all children there will be times when you have to show him who the boss is. Capricorn has this thing about being in charge in every situation, so don't be surprised when your child challenges your authority. You might be quite sure that it's naptime, for example, but Capricorn will insist he doesn't need to go to sleep—or get dressed—or take a bath . . . . If you give in to these objections, you'll soon find that your little goat will continue to take on more territory. Do you really want to have macaroni and cheese or chicken fingers every night for dinner?

Capricorn's demanding side will take shape around his friends, too, and your child may take on an "Executive Suite" approach to simple relationships. Don't micromanage every incident that goes down in the playground, but do monitor young Capricorn's friendships to ensure they're not all in existence just so your child can dominate others. Introduce your child to some older relatives or neighborhood kids so he can find out what it's like not to be the smartest, the strongest, and the bossiest one around.

✳ DISCIPLINE ✳

Capricorn needs to learn that there is a hierarchy in most life situations, and, in her world, you're the one in the superior position. When Capricorn gets angry about not being allowed to do things or go places that are not age-appropriate, you will have to offer more discipline than sympathy.

In order to ensure you remain the dominant force in the household, you'll have to be creative about discipline. When your child is haughty with a friend or sassy toward you, test her basic interpersonal and management skills, and make sure she understands that everyone has things that they need to learn. You can insist that, before Capricorn can come out of time out, she show the capability to master tasks that are menial and "beneath" what she perceives to be her station in life. Then, an apology for the transgression can be accepted and all can be forgiven. Humility is perhaps the most important—and difficult—virtue for Capricorn to learn, and some mild form of "being knocked down a notch" is the best way for your child to understand how crucial it is.

Your Capricorn child is really of two minds about her precocious way of being. While she is certain that her peers are not worthy equals, there's also a little bit of jealousy about not being like all the other kids. The goat's difficulty in fitting in stems from the fact she doesn't believe that other people are worthy of being trusted. To educate Capricorn on the importance of collaboration, you might want to present opportunities for your child to be part of a group. Merit-based activities such as scouting and martial arts are good for Capricorn, even if she doesn't want to participate at first.

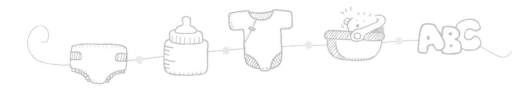

FAVORITE THINGS

SING THESE SONGS WITH YOUR CAPRICORN CHILD

› **"This Old Man":** Capricorn likes the thought of an older, wiser persona.

› **"Old McDonald":** This baby will always be assessing what someone has.

› **"Five Little Monkeys":** A moralistic tale of why Capricorn isn't a very silly child.

WATCH MOVIES LIKE THIS WITH YOUR CAPRICORN CHILD

› *The Wizard of Oz:* There's not much that Capricorn wouldn't give to be the "One Behind the Curtain."

› *A Boy Named Charlie Brown:* The wry humor will appeal to Capricorn, and the lesson of picking up and trying again after a failure will prepare your child for reality.

› *Baby's Day Out:* Capricorn will have no trouble believing that it's possible to thwart a kidnapping plot without adult supervision.

PLAY THESE GAMES WITH YOUR CAPRICORN CHILD

› **Red Rover:** Early practice at hiring competent staff.

› **Marbles:** Capricorn will enjoy winning them from his peers.

› **Simon Says:** This is where Capricorn learns how to manage human resources.

READ THESE BOOKS, RHYMES, AND FAIRY TALES TO YOUR CAPRICORN CHILD

› **"Rip Van Winkle":** Encourages Capricorn to avoid separating from the mainstream.

› **"This Little Pig":** Right away, Capricorn knows he wants to be the one that gets the roast beef.

› **"The Golden Goose":** A bit of instruction for Capricorn to avoid getting too greedy.

TREAT YOUR CAPRICORN CHILD TO THESE FOODS

› **Roast Beef:** Plain and simple, that's this baby's style.

› **Potatoes:** Goes right with that roast beef!

› **Peas:** Simple, economical, and smoosh-able.

✳ CAPRICORN'S BABY STYLE ✳

Plain and simple, yet elegant—that will be Capricorn's style from cradle to college and beyond.

GIRLS: Young Capricorn girls could display a preference for designer fashion. This can be fine as long as you make sure that what your little goat is wearing is age appropriate.

BOYS: Never dress your Capricorn boy in anything that isn't dignified and plain. Little Capricorn isn't about fun hats or strange colors. Don't worry about his love of black clothing—it's a Capricorn thing!

✳ CAPRICORN'S ENVIRONMENT ✳

Organization and simplicity are two Capricorn necessities. If you can, provide your baby with furniture that has simple lines, and few—if any—ornate decorations. There can be a few baby-like things in the nursery, but too much clutter will definitely spark little Capricorn's rather noticeable voice of discontentment.

✳ CALMING CAPRICORN ✳

Capricorn cries out of frustration more than anything else. Remember that even while he is a child your little Capricorn wants to be a grownup! If he only knew what being an adult was like maybe you wouldn't have to try to explain why that's not possible, and how it's better to wait for certain things. Still, letting him feel like a person is the best way to calm your Capricorn. If your baby is lying down, pick him up and place his body in a sitting or standing position, using your discretion as to how much weight your baby can bear. Feeling more "grown-up" and being included in what you're doing will always make your Capricorn baby feel more serene.

✳ STIMULATING CAPRICORN ✳

Capricorn isn't the kind of child who will sit around and do nothing for very long. You're going to have to keep your little goat busy with toys that engage his mind and gratify his ego.

- **Interlocking Blocks:** Even Capricorn girls have a thing for building towers and fantasize about owning a penthouse apartment with a view of Central Park
- **Drawing Tools:** From a simple pad and crayon to an Etch A Sketch or small computer, your Capricorn enjoys creating inventions and drawing up plans.
- **Music Player:** Your Capricorn child may display musical talent at some point, and you can foster this by allowing your child to choose the tunes he wants to hear. Be sure to include some of the classics; the intricacy of the symphony orchestra intrigues Capricorn babies.

✳ CAPRICORN'S LEARNING STYLE ✳

Capricorn learns by watching and listening, and by competing with peers and teachers to see who has really become the "master" of the task at hand. Capricorn's biggest obstacle to learning is the misconception that she already knows everything. Discipline and deference are important things for your child to develop. If you get calls from the school, they will probably either be to congratulate you on raising such a genius or because your child refuses to accept the authority of her teacher. There will be times when teachers aren't actually "right," but your little Capricorn needs to learn how to deal with this.

PARENTING CAPRICORN

If your sign is . . .

ARIES

You'll be proud of your Capricorn, but you'll also sense what a responsibility it will be to raise your baby right. Your Capricorn child will probably try to prove who's smarter, faster, or better at a certain skill, but as the parent, you can't get embroiled in this kind of battle. Capricorn might not be as physically oriented as you are, but she will be sharper than you might realize. Even as a small tyke, this child will find ways out of doing chores and will use her ingenuity to make them easier. Sometimes this power of invention might not be so healthy, but it will always be practical—at least from her standpoint! Encourage Capricorn to get involved in more activities outdoors. She'll get hooked on the idea of running, playing, and trying to see who can shoot the most baskets.

When you play with Capricorn down on her level, you'll see what an intellectual powerhouse this child can be. Although you might be bigger and stronger, this child was born with the knowledge and determination it takes to survive. Nurture this by teaching Capricorn that it's okay to have free time, and more than fine to just have fun.

TAURUS

You and your little Capricorn will enjoy spending time together, and your baby will appreciate the warm and comfortable home you are more than happy to provide. You'll be glad Capricorn doesn't ask for a lot of your time, and you'll be happy to hold your little one when he needs a bit of reassurance.

On the whole, the two of you can have a very warm relationship that's quite like a nice friendship. Still, you're going to have to wrestle with Capricorn's tendency to take over, whether it's appropriate or not. Although it might be tempting to skip a nap or give an extra cookie, you know caving to Capricorn's every demand isn't really the best thing you can do for your child. Little does your child know that he's dealing with the most hard-nosed negotiator imaginable, but you can remind Capricorn of this when you refuse to give in and allow him to bend the rules of the roost.

GEMINI

This little one will seem so serious, you'll wonder if there's something bothering him! Chances are your highly evolved and exceptionally intelligent child simply refuses to be the one who you want to squeeze and play with all the time. Capricorn has an old soul, and despite efforts to gain your respect will provide you with more than a few reasons to smile.

The key to your relationship lies in giving this child the kind of support and strong boundaries that he needs to grow to his full potential. This isn't all that easy for you to do, but if you want your little Capricorn to feel safe, you're going to have to do it! Otherwise, you could end up with a child whose desire to take charge knows no bounds—especially when it's time to pick up all of your little goat's toys. Use your wit and your unpredictability to keep this child guessing, and you'll gain control of the situation—and get the appropriate amount of respect, as well.

CANCER

You might be worried about doing "enough" for your little Capricorn, but you needn't be concerned at all. Despite your differences, your child will appreciate the things you do to create a warm and safe environment where she can grow up. Your instincts for what your little goat needs and wants will be useful throughout infancy, and your child will sense that you truly do know what's best in any given situation.

Your Capricorn might, as time goes on, take up a protective posture toward you. It's not that she doesn't think you can take care of yourself, but rather because she honors her responsibility to your family almost as much as you do; the concept of "parent" is very sacred and Capricorn will make sure no one hurts you or gets in your way. Of course, it's not your child's job to look out for your safety, but you'll have to agree that the efforts little Capricorn makes in that regard are very cute and special.

Give your Capricorn a lot of responsibilities around the house. Although she might not want to learn how to cook and clean, these are life skills that everyone eventually needs. Capricorn will respect your abilities and strive to do things "almost" as well as you.

LEO

You and your Capricorn are a lot more similar than you might think when you first encounter this serious little soul. While you are outgoing and straightforward about your humor, Capricorn is reserved and very dry when it comes to devising ways to get laughs. Yet the two of you share a very important role—that of "leader." In some ways, it might seem like your Capricorn is trying to dominate you, and you'll probably wonder why he dares to do this.

Capricorn can be pretty bossy, and when your child shows you the point he's trying to make, you'll likely agree that his view makes a whole lot of sense. You might think it's cute at first, but eventually Capricorn will overdo it and force you to step in and show your child who the boss really is. When this occurs, there's no need to be overly brusque about it. Remember that despite Capricorn's strong and seemingly insensitive bravado, there is a very quiet and gentle energy at work there. Teach your child that the respect that comes with being a leader isn't a matter of entitlement. It must be earned. Then make sure you provide an excellent example!

VIRGO

You and your Capricorn will have a wonderful time bonding through your child's infancy. Compliant and quiet, your little one will respond well to your orderly environment and be grateful for your organized nature. At times you may wonder why your baby isn't interested in the cute little toys you buy or the stories you want to tell, but eventually you'll come to accept how your child's personality is far more mature and advanced than average.

You can foster this by giving your child some more meaty and stimulating activities to enjoy. The two of you share the affinity for the "element" earth, and you are both practical and down to earth when it comes to your ideas and favorite things to do. This child might love building a terrarium or apprenticing as you work on some of your more advanced handicrafts. While Capricorn doesn't share your love of details, your little goat does have the ability to see the grand overview of things. You might learn a lot from seeing things through your child's eyes, but it's more important for you to share what you know about the importance of covering all your bases. That way, when Capricorn hits those home runs, they will really count.

LIBRA

The quiet and unassuming Capricorn baby will be a welcome addition to your home and you won't have to worry about an overload of disruptions to your equilibrium and routine. All parenting experiences are as much a learning process as they are anything else, and in your case raising Capricorn is going to be a lesson in becoming more decisive. Your equivocation over where to eat or what to wear won't be easily tolerated by your Capricorn child, especially as he grows. You'll have to ask if you think you would respect someone who has so much difficulty making a decision, and then remember just how demanding Capricorn can be when it comes to building trust and respect. Then you must rise to the occasion and be grateful that without even knowing it, your little goat makes you more aware of how you can improve your own skills for coping with daily life.

SCORPIO

You will adore raising your little goat because you'll know exactly what he needs and have no fear about providing it. Capricorn children are quiet at first, but their intelligence and maturity is so profound that it can be hard to remember they are still very small and inexperienced. Capricorns will try to impose a schedule upon you and use the "power" of making noise and raising concerns about their welfare to make sure you stick to it.

Lucky for you—and for this rather clever child—you're far too smart to fall for that. You'll know right away that what Capricorn needs most is guidance, love, and restrictions. Without imposing your way on this child, neither of you will have an easy time of it. In order to grow into the fine leader he will one day be, it's necessary for Capricorn to learn about the rules, what they are, and how to either work with them or find a way around them. Watch your child closely—and of course you will!—and you'll be able to guide him through society's labyrinth with your calm ways. Your Capricorn child will love you for it.

SAGITTARIUS

You'll be excited to meet your Capricorn child, but don't expect your baby to be brimming with as much enthusiasm and bounciness as you! The Capricorn child is far more reserved than most, and if you don't learn how to match her level of involvement or excitement about an activity, could become rather upset. Because you're every bit as smart as your child, though, you know you've been given this little Capricorn so that you could teach her the joy of life.

Capricorn is more than capable of having a good time; in fact, you might catch your child indulging in guilty pleasures now and again. Watch your little one count the money in her piggy bank, or witness the pure enjoyment she gets from indulging in a favorite food. Capricorn has all the same emotions you or anyone else does—it is just not in the Capricorn constitution to show them.

Knowing this will make being Capricorn's parent far less stressful. Keep a strong sense of your own authority, but also give Capricorn the greatest gift of all: knowing that it's okay to cry when you're hurt and be serious when you should—but it's just as important to laugh and be happy.

CAPRICORN

You might want to send out for business cards with your and your Capricorn's name on them the moment your beautiful baby is born, but it might be better to wait a while! You and your Capricorn child will have no problem understanding one another; you'll have similar moods and the same tendency not to show your emotions overtly. Still, it will be impossible to not soften when you see your little Capricorn smile your way. You might think you know what he's really thinking, but don't be so sure of yourself.

Because your child is so much like you, there could easily be a struggle for dominance that develops very early in life. You might think you have it all under control when you suddenly realize that your little Capricorn has pulled a number on you! It won't surprise you to see this happen; at least it shouldn't! Still, it's going to take a lot of self-examination to raise this baby in the best possible way.

The best thing you can teach your Capricorn child is to have integrity and to realize that power without such a virtue is an empty prize. Put simply, when you respect people they have a far easier time respecting you.

AQUARIUS

You'll be thrilled with your little Capricorn because you can tell at the outset there won't be too many tears and it will be fairly easy to relate to this rather pragmatic little child. You'll be a good parent for Capricorn as long as you can stave off this child's attempts to take over your household. There's no doubt that your little Capricorn is well-behaved; but what you might not know is how assertive—and sometimes aggressive—he can be. When you first watch your child play with others, you'll notice how they seem to defer to his leadership. This isn't because Capricorn is doing anything "bad," but you'll have to make sure it stays that way. Sometimes, Capricorn children will strive to attain power over other people, even when it doesn't rightly belong to them.

The biggest lesson you'll teach your little Capricorn is that the goal isn't always to control other people or make power grabs. The welfare of everyone, especially the larger community, is even more important. If you can achieve this, you will help to foster someone who is sure to combine ability, determination, and social compassion in order to do incredible things. Just by raising your little goat in that way you'll make the world a better place.

PISCES

You'll be amazed by your little Capricorn's advanced state of being. Your baby won't even seem like an infant because she will be looking around and taking in the environment like a child at least a few years older. Your child's confidence and inner strength will be a marvel to you because these things don't always come naturally to you.

If you're worried that you're not the "right" parent for a child with so much determination, you're wrong! You're the perfect person to help your little Capricorn work on the things that he needs to improve upon. For instance, your child can be less imaginative and whimsical than other children. While you must accept this, you can also try to help him open up his more vulnerable and fanciful side by establishing utter trust between the two of you. Part of this will entail running a much tighter ship than you normally would, though. Capricorn will demand order and predictability—two items that you don't come by without some hard work. Still, if you want to enlighten this child you may have to do some work on yourself—and that's part of the miracle of being a parent!

CHAPTER 11

Aquarius:

The Lovable Oddball

BORN BETWEEN: January 21–February 20
RULING PLANET: Saturn – The daytime, strong and stubborn side
EXALTED PLANET: None needed. Aquarius's single-mindedness is just as steadfast
as Saturn.
COLOR: Orange, Teal
GEMSTONES: Aquamarine and Herderite

THE LITTLE BABY WITH THE CURIOUS LOOK AND FARAWAY EYES is indeed a dreamer! Born during the height of winter when the world tends to stay inside, your little Aquarius believes that it's important to care about the welfare of others, and to build a community that protects everyone. Your water-bearer baby will amaze you with the ideas he comes up with over the years, and you'll have a lot of fun raising this brilliant child. Aquarius is an *air* sign, and is also *fixed*, which is part of the reason why your child is so steadfastly sure that his ideas are the only ones worth thinking about. You may want to show Aquarius the "right" way to do something, but your child will deliberately invent a "new" way and rebel against convention at every turn.

Each Aquarius individual believes it is his job to bring light and knowledge to the world. With this mission, Aquarius also must believe that the world we have right now needs some alterations. That is why your child, more so than others, will disregard authority, try to revise the way you do things, and for the most part, turn your world on its ear!

Aquarius children are thinkers, talkers, *and* doers, and they will usually try to find unique ways of expressing themselves. Emotionally, your child won't be the warmest, but with your help will open up to expressing feelings more openly. Give your little Aquarius affection even when he doesn't ask for it—just because. When you do this, he'll begin to realize there are bonds that can be built that don't involve thoughts or words. You'll have a great opportunity to do this during your baby's infancy, but after that it will become more difficult. What are you waiting for? Give that baby extra kisses and caresses while you still can!

✳ YOUR AQUARIUS BOY ✳

Aquarius boys are exceptionally endearing. They have a curiosity that almost never fails to make the rest of us laugh. Not particularly physically active or even inclined toward sports, most Aquarius boys will seek to understand the mysteries of the world, beginning with their own bodies and then progressing to the world around them. This is the little boy who will eat worms just to find out what they taste like and make mixtures of food and spices in your sink so he can come up with "magic potions."

Your Aquarius boy isn't fond of the idea of having his freedom restricted, by you or anyone else. If you allow him to get away with doing whatever he wants, you'll put his safety as well as your sanity at risk. He'll construct arguments in favor of his doing something hazardous at a much younger age than he should be allowed that are almost impossible to argue with. That is why you must not give him the opportunity to argue. You have to build a very thick skin to deal with his rebellious nature, but you must also keep a very strict set of rules around certain activities and behavior. If Aquarius doesn't comply with your wishes, then you will have to know how to make him more manageable. This has more to do with giving him freedom than it does taking it away, but you must be able to grab and retain control over the way freedom is doled out to your Aquarius boy.

As he grows older, your Aquarius boy will display an interest in the sciences and possibly gravitate toward engineering, particularly information technology. Aquarius enjoys dealing in the world of ideas, but unless these ideas can be used to make the world a better place, your Aquarius boy will lose interest.

If your Aquarius boy is especially compassionate, he could develop a strong interest in areas such as the environmental sciences, biology, and animal advocacy. Prepare to respond to your Aquarius's requests to prepare special meals and to try new ways of celebrating holidays. Your Aquarius boy will assert himself by attempting to get you to change your ways. While you can indulge his whims within reason, don't let him turn the household upside-down. The real world will not be so accommodating, and he must learn to compromise. He will most definitely *try* to convert you to his way of seeing things, but standing strong to give him the impression that the world will require a certain amount of compliance is probably a good idea.

YOUR AQUARIUS GIRL

Your little Aquarius girl will be very special! You'll know right away that there's something about her that makes her different from the rest of the children her age, and when you forget how unusual she can be, she's bound to remind you. As an infant, she'll seem to be very wise and give you the feeling she has an "old soul." As she grows, she'll be a very lively child with a penchant for doing things that draw attention to her. Although she might not want to be the "class clown," she certainly wants to be seen as the pied piper.

Your Aquarius girl will have certain ideas that she wants other people to learn about. Most of them will have to do with making the world "a better place." She'll relate quite easily to rescuing animals, preventing pollution, and encouraging recycling. Don't be surprised if she even comes up with ways of protecting the earth that you haven't heard of, or that you haven't taught her about. She just is always thinking about what's best for everyone.

This doesn't mean she doesn't think about her own needs, though. Aquarius is quite sure of herself and she also doesn't suffer fools very easily. She is rather bold and doesn't lack in self-esteem. When it comes to competing with others, including boys, her attitude is that she doesn't ask for her "rights"—she just takes them! Woe to anyone who tries to stop her, too. The "fixed" nature of her sign makes her very stubborn. She sets her mind to something, does it, and then wants to know why everyone else doesn't do it too. It's never enough for your daughter to simply blaze a trail. No matter how out of the ordinary her way of seeing a situation might be, she'll always insist that's she's right, and everyone else is unenlightened.

In case you were wondering, you will fall into that category from time to time, too. It's important to understand that your little girl's development must take the path of separating from you, perhaps more vehemently than other children do with their parents. Hang tough and be proud of her for becoming who she's supposed to be—a strong, individualistic woman whose futuristic vision of the world will probably, in some way, make it a way better place.

TALENTS AND AFFINITIES

SCIENCE

Your little Aquarius will be very curious about how the world is put together. This is the baby who will try to take the rattle apart to see why it makes so much noise when he shakes it! You'll always have to have one eye on what your little Aquarius is doing to both keep him out of danger and dote on his total genius!

LANGUAGE

Aquarius wants to communicate, but only on her terms. Your little one will work hard to learn how to talk, but once she learns that skill don't expect her to answer your requests in the way you'd like. Aquarius is just as likely to reinvent names for things so she can make you learn what they are—in an attempt to put your roles in reverse.

ACTIVISM

Your little Aquarius child will be a politically minded little thing, acutely aware of what's going on in the world and eager to share opinions with all who will listen. As your child grows, encourage community work and also school politics so he can learn about the work that goes on behind the scenes and get involved.

FAVORITE THINGS

SING THESE SONGS WITH YOUR AQUARIUS CHILD

› **"The More We Get Together":** Aquarius's group consciousness will rise up early.

› **"Kumbaya":** Making peace with everyone so we can all live together.

› **"Wheels on the Bus":** Early sociological observations of a common urban activity.

WATCH MOVIES LIKE THESE WITH YOUR AQUARIUS CHILD

› *Ice Age:* Aquarius will admire this tale of tribal loyalty and perseverance.

› *Cool Runnings:* This story of a team that wins the battle of equality will validate Aquarius's sensibilities.

› *The Adventures of Milo and Otis:* Two totally different kinds of creatures can find lots in common and help one another out. Aquarius is born knowing this is truth.

PLAY THESE GAMES WITH YOUR AQUARIUS CHILD

› **Blind Man's Bluff:** To Aquarius, everyone is the same anyway.

› **Duck, Duck, Goose:** A good way for Aquarius to choose up some capable deputy organizers.

› **Hot Lava:** Plays to Aquarius's imagination and that sense of communal effort.

READ THESE BOOKS, RHYMES, AND FAIRY TALES TO YOUR AQUARIUS CHILD

› *The Three Musketeers:* "All for one, one for all . . ."

› **"Humpty Dumpty":** The King isn't invulnerable . . . see?

› **"The Frog Prince":** Everyone has the potential to be a fine leader.

TREAT YOUR AQUARIUS CHILD TO THESE FOODS

› **Rice Pasta:** Light on Aquarius's system and unusual enough to appeal.

› **Coconut Juice:** Not easy to find, but that could be why Aquarius will love it.

› **Okra:** Aquarius will love something everyone else hates.

LITTLE CHALLENGES

The Aquarius child, for all her little quirks, is a wonderful child to raise. While you'll ultimately be very proud of your child's achievements as an individual, you might also have to deal with a lot of the growing pains that come with such an independent-minded and contrarian child.

Some of the most difficult moments might come when you try to get your little Aquarius to conform to the constructs of school life. It's a good idea to find a place that encourages individual achievement, but if you're restricted to one that is very conventional, you'll have to teach Aquarius to work within the constraints of authority. The reward will be the knowledge Aquarius prizes so highly.

DISCIPLINE

It really isn't possible to keep Aquarius "in line" all the time, but you'll have to administer some lessons now and again. To keep your child safe and well-equipped for life on her own in the future, you have to balance your enforcement of the rules with an allowance for freedom.

Perhaps the best way to instill the right combination of attributes into your child is to teach that old adage, "With every freedom comes a responsibility." Start young with your Aquarius. If he takes out a bunch of toys, that's a "freedom." The "responsibility" is to treat the toys nicely and to put them away when playtime is over. This might seem trite, but setting that in your Aquarius child's mind is going to give you a lot to build on in later years.

When Aquarius doesn't live up to the responsibility, then he can no longer have the freedom. You must be very strict about enforcing this. For example, if Aquarius fails to return the building blocks to their box, you remove them from the play area and place them somewhere Aquarius cannot access. There may be some screaming and yelling, but you can do it. Aquarius can have the blocks or whatever else you remove (including car keys when that time comes) after there has been an acknowledgment of wrongdoing and a promise that it won't happen again.

It would be ideal to get an apology from your Aquarius child, but it will be a long time coming! If you can be patient and persistent enough to hold out, you will be doing your Aquarius child a big favor by teaching him the value of saying "I'm sorry," and gaining forgiveness.

✳ AQUARIUS'S BABY STYLE ✳

Kooky. Yes, really! This is the child who invented the idea of wearing mismatched socks.

GIRLS: She'll pick out a bunch of clothes that don't seem to go together at all and wind up wearing a unique and beautiful outfit.

BOYS: He'll pick out futuristic-looking clothing and will be persistent about wearing superhero undies. Sometimes, your Aquarius boy thinks he really is from outer space.

✳ AQUARIUS'S ENVIRONMENT ✳

Aquarius doesn't really care much about what her nursery is like as long as you're there to provide basic services and there is adequate space to stretch out. Quirky objects and wild, bright colors will please your little water-bearer, though.

CALMING AQUARIUS

Because Aquarius can be so stubborn, there will be times when she cries so hard that you don't think the noise will ever stop. Most of the time, taking care of the basics, such as food, diapers, and physical contact will calm Aquarius down, as will some time being free to kick on a blanket or play with a mobile or another object that she can use to create movement.

Aquarius will also be easily distracted by TV and movies, but use this tactic judiciously. Because her fixed nature creates such intense focus, and there is a slight tendency toward becoming obsessed, too much TV could turn your child into a media junkie—and that really isn't what you want to do for a child with such a superior mind! Use Aquarius's fine mind to your advantage when she is upset, and read rhymes or tell stories. Some ambient music could also soothe Aquarius's nerves.

STIMULATING AQUARIUS

Aquarius is very interested in the world, so it's not hard to get your baby's brain engaged. Your little water-bearer will love these toys:

- **Electronic "Talking" Toys and Books:** These let Aquarius learn firsthand about cause and effect.
- **Dress-Up Clothes:** Both boys and girls will have a "superhero complex" that needs feeding.
- **A City or Farm Play Set:** These allow Aquarius to develop that emerging sense of social consciousness.

AQUARIUS' LEARNING STYLE

Aquarius learns best in a group setting; your child needs the camaraderie of classmates in order to feel as though what is being learned has relevance. He won't see anything the way the rest of the world does so prepare to find original ways of presenting new learning material. Your Aquarius may not do well in school if he is forced to comply with a set method of learning; instead, he needs the right balance between freedom and structure and as much exposure to technology as possible.

PARENTING AQUARIUS

If your sign is . . .

ARIES

You and Aquarius are going to have an interesting tug of war. You're very physical, your child is more mentally attuned, and the two of you look at the world from two vastly different perspectives. While you believe it's important to get what you want in life, your child is constantly looking to how the greater community can benefit from what she does. The one thing you can agree on is the importance of the self. You and your little Aquarius will probably spend a lot of time adjusting to one another, but throughout this exercise you're going to have to remember you're the one in charge.

It's far too easy for you to become embroiled in a head-to-head fight, especially with someone who is as single-minded as your Aquarius child. While she is young, it's important to let your Aquarius know that you respect her individuality, but you need to insist on getting respect and deference if you're going to help your child learn how to take that big sense of self and find a way to make it fit into society. While you teach Aquarius about merging with the rest of humanity, your child will teach you to act like the grownup you need to be as a parent.

TAURUS

Even though you're rather conventional and your little water-bearer is anything but, the two of you will get along much better than you might imagine. You'll think the ideas that your child comes up with are wonderful and original, and you'll be very proud of the way he chooses activities and sticks to them until they're mastered. Meanwhile, you'll provide a steady and prosperous life for your little Aquarius, who will depend on you for feedback about the nobility and and honor of his ideas. Aquarius will also look at you as a challenge; if he can persuade you to change your mind the rest of the world will be a piece of cake!

Always give your Aquarius child lots of room when it comes to choosing friends or fields of study. You might think Aquarius would make a wonderful accountant, but Aquarius would probably rather not be tied down to considerations that encompass just the material world. Expose your Aquarius child to as much science and technology as possible and make sure some kind of activity in his life includes opportunities for exercising a grandiosity of heart. For example, loving animals and doing nice things for the less fortunate will balance the cool calculation of Aquarius's rational mind. Lucky for Aquarius, you'll set the perfect example.

GEMINI

Your little Aquarius will amaze you with her ability to connect with you even before she has learned to talk. This child has landed into the right pair of arms, because you intuitively pick up what's on Aquarius's mind, and later on you'll think whatever your child is thinking or talking about is really cool. The two of you have a natural affinity for the life of the mind, and even though you use it in different ways you have a mutual appreciation. In addition, your Aquarius child is lucky to have you because you possess the ability to relate to people and the courage to connect with just about anyone who comes into your sight.

Teach Aquarius to develop more sensitivity to others and help her to work with the idea of "charm." Your child didn't come equipped with the kind of tolerance for others that you have and needs to learn how to extend her personality so she can get along better with other people. Yes, it's true that Aquarius seeks out ways to be the "oddball," but at the same time she would be very lonely without a few friends. Although your little Aquarius has no desire to know as many people as you do, you'll be able to show her how to bring at least a few trusted comrades into her life, for which she'll be very grateful! For that alone, your Aquarius child will open up and embrace you as one of her best friends ever.

CANCER

Your little Aquarius child will be an enigma to you from the first time you meet. Still, you'll adore your infant and will work as you always do to give him everything that's needed for a happy and secure life. The biggest difference between the two of you will be your way of seeing the world around you through your emotions, and your Aquarius baby's apparent detachment from his emotions. Your little Aquarius certainly has feelings; he just tends to put them aside to try to reason out the situation at hand.

In order to establish yourself as the ultimate authority for your child, you'll have to take the attitude of "turn the other cheek." Your Aquarius, even before he is able to talk, will seem to reject your attempts to show and share affection. You'll certainly have to shield yourself from these rebuffs and put aside the idea that your baby isn't nuzzling with you because Aquarius doesn't love you. As part of your parent-child pact, your little Aquarius will come to learn to pay at least a little bit more attention to his emotional being, and you'll come to realize you can love someone without constantly looking to that individual for reassurance and emotional support.

LEO

The joy of having an Aquarius will strike you the first time you hold your little one and will continue for the rest of her life. Positioned on opposite sides of the zodiac wheel, you and Aquarius have a special tie. You have many of the talents and attributes that are missing in Aquarius's personality, and Aquarius has many things to teach you. As in all parent-child situations, it's important to remember you must establish and maintain your authority without becoming dictatorial. Still, your little Aquarius will need you to provide certain restrictions so he will learn how to integrate into the rest of the world.

Give your Aquarius challenges, and make them of the sort that bring out his compassion for others. Although Aquarius seems to think a lot about "the world at large," developing individual warmth can be somewhat difficult. You'll teach this by example, most certainly, but you must also provide Aquarius with direct, logical ways of learning why this is important. A pet might be a great way to teach this lesson—and this would also allow you to demonstrate your awesome ability to bring the best out in any creature you encounter, even your stridently different, always unusual Aquarius child.

VIRGO

Having an Aquarius will be a blessing to you but at times this child will be challenging. Your little Aquarius will do all she can to draw that line between herself and you. This will work out fine in the end, but the kind of close bonding you were hoping for could be elusive with this intellectually oriented child.

As a baby, Aquarius won't need all the fussy things that you want to do to make your infant's life more comfortable. While you're trying to keep her hands extra-clean, your toddler is very likely to ask you to keep your sanitary wet wipe to yourself!

Aquarius will put you to the test as a child by stubbornly refusing to succumb to your directions, and it will only get more difficult as her astute mind grows and develops. Before you know it, Aquarius will be presenting logical arguments to every precept and custom you put forth. You might say "An apple a day keeps the doctor away," and then get a lecture on how some fruits and vegetables have poisons on them.

LIBRA

Life with your little Aquarius will be a laugh a minute. This child's offbeat ways will amuse you and provide fodder for endless family in-jokes. Yet while everybody's laughing, your little Aquarius will just continue to be who he is! The most amazing thing about this child is how little concern there is for the opinions and judgments of others. This is certainly something you can learn about and integrate into your own life—but before you get to that, maybe you'd better think about how you're going to handle little Aquarius and avoid allowing this live wire to take over your whole household.

You're going to have to leave some leeway so your child can have the freedom he cherishes so dearly, but you're going to have to keep a close eye on this little water-bearer. Aquarius is extremely curious and will want to know what it feels like to touch that $500 vase you have in the living room and what would happen after it gets tipped off the table by a tiny hand. Aquarius's lack of concern for beauty will get to you, but you'll gladly give up any aesthetic connections for the happy-go-lucky, pleasant relationship the two of you will share.

SCORPIO

Your relationship with your little Aquarius will be very deep, but you'll be far more conscious of what's going on than your little child will be. Always striving to stand out from the crowd, the Aquarius child is going to go out of her way to shock you. Because you have so much insight and work on such profound instinct, though, you won't let this affect a thing. In fact, your child will be surprised to note how little there is that actually gets you upset.

It pays to show your Aquarius child you care about him, though, because even this seemingly impervious child deserves and needs that kind of attention. Little Aquarius just won't show it! Although the two of you seem very different, in fact you share a very strong bond. You are both very set in your ways of doing things and you want to do all that you set out to accomplish as well as you possibly can. You're far too wise to allow this child to avoid complying with society to some degree, but you'll also advocate for Aquarius because you so deeply believe your child is here to enrich and enlighten this world.

SAGITTARIUS

You'll be thrilled to meet your little water-bearer and very curious to know what she wants and expects from your relationship. Since Aquarius is even more strident about being "free" than you are, you need to allow your child to have some freedom but be smart enough to keep watch over your little one, too. That won't be so hard, because you'll totally enjoy watching your baby discover the world. You'll probably also want to come along for some of the adventures—but at some point, Aquarius will want to cut you loose! Pay attention to this rather valuable lesson; it can help you become a lot more sensitive to the way other people feel when you flit off to who-knows-where once again.

Little Aquarius will always try to be different from other people, including you. You'll admire your child's originality and delight in watching how quickly she picks up the developmental skills related to intelligence and analysis.

CAPRICORN

That little Aquarius you're holding will give you much joy and satisfaction, but that will only come after years of hard work. You and Aquarius are a lot alike, but you will likely be at odds much of the time. You will love your Aquarius child, but you'll be very confused about where she gets her ideas. Your little water-bearer will love you, too, especially after you devise ways of getting Aquarius to respect you and follow your lead.

Aquarius is always bucking the system, so you will probably cringe as you watch your child try to reinvent just about every childhood institution. You must accept that this is what your child will do, under almost any circumstances, and then come to see these moments as teaching—and learning—opportunities. Aquarius will make you a better parent by challenging you and never accepting the answer "Because I said so." Your little Aquarius will also show you the importance of daring to ask "Why?"

AQUARIUS

Having a child that's just like you can be a thrilling experience for most parents, but for you it's going to be quite a challenge! After all, aren't *you* the one who's a total original? Why is your child not doing things the way you think they should be done, and when will your little Aquarius learn that there are rules that must be obeyed?

If your parents are around to see, you'll have to pardon them while they get a few laughs out of watching you raise a child who's so much like you . . . it seems to drive you nuts (but in a good way!). Your little Aquarius, just like you, is born to blaze a trail that makes him unique. As you know, this one-of-a-kind personality is necessary so that your Aquarius can lead others to see a vision of the world they might never notice and his clever, socially conscious, and utterly individual personality will point the way.

You'll learn so much from the experience of raising your Aquarius child. Not only will you become enamored with the way he takes on the world, you'll come to appreciate your own uniqueness and grow in the knowledge that by doing things your way you've established a precedent your child is certain to follow, when that time comes. Meanwhile, all you need to do is love your little Aquarius.

PISCES

You and your little water-bearer have an odd connection that doesn't make sense to anyone but the two of you. While you're holding this child in your arms, you will think of all the hopes and dreams you have for her, but what she wants is bound to be different than what you have in mind! The good news is that this will bother you less than it might bother other parents. This will make your Aquarius child very happy!

You have so much to offer this baby—not because you're the most organized, strategic, or well-prepared parent—but because you accept your little Aquarius for the unique individual he really is. Also, the universal love you each share for humankind bonds you in the notion of finding ways to improve life for every creature on the planet.

CHAPTER 12

Pisces:

Wide-Eyed and Wonderful

BORN BETWEEN: February 21–March 20
RULING PLANET: Jupiter – The more heartfelt, spiritual, and boundless nighttime side
EXALTED PLANET: Venus
COLOR: Lilac and Sky Blue
GEMSTONES: Amethyst and Moldavite

Y OUR PISCES BABY DRIFTED INTO YOUR LIFE at the time winter was ending and spring was about to arrive, which means that this child will always remind you there is a reason for being here and there is always the hope of renewal and redemption. Pisces is a *water* sign, and it's of the *mutable* nature. Because of this your little Pisces is deeply emotional and spiritual, and so intuitive that you'll swear your child is a born psychic. From the time of his birth, you'll watch your fish tap in on a certain unknown force, and you may come to see that this is the way Pisces sees the world.

Compassionate, loving, and without boundaries, yours is a very special child, but one who will also need your help very, very much.

Pisces isn't very good at drawing lines between where the fantasy world ends and the real world begins. This is where you can help. You can allow your Pisces child to be entertained by and engaged in fantasies of all kinds, but it's up to you to explain that real life doesn't always work that way. You'll need to work hard with Pisces to get your child to be more organized and structured about the way he goes about performing certain tasks. Pisces will have a tendency to start something, and then get distracted by something else. Help Pisces by suggesting he sing a song or count to ten while washing hands or brushing teeth to ensure that he follows through. And always make sure that you show Pisces that you have boundaries and are capable of protecting yourself from people taking advantage of you—including your little Pisces. This valuable lesson will help your child build his character and become the highly evolved, creative and imaginative individual he was meant to be.

✳ YOUR PISCES BOY ✳

Pisces boys are very quiet and gentle as a rule, and they won't seem to be as rough and rowdy as the other boys. However, this doesn't mean that your son will lack masculinity or that he won't have other areas of life where he is extremely active and assertive. Your little Pisces will also display a great talent for the creative arts. He will sing to himself, draw pictures, and even dance—whether there's music playing in the background or not!

Your Pisces son may also be especially attracted to fairy tales and fantasy stories that allow him to be seen as a hero, a prince, or a knight in shining armor. Pisces wants to save the world, whether it's by scaling tall buildings or wiping the tears of a damsel in distress. He'll need to feel as though this is possible, to some degree, because his life's work will probably involve this sort of activity one day, maybe as a doctor, an EMT, or an advocacy lawyer. In the meantime, you have to create a sense of true reality for your Pisces son, too. He'll have to realize that it isn't always possible to "save" someone, and that it isn't always the best thing for that other person to be saved.

While it isn't easy to explain in a young boy's terms why it's not always good to sacrifice oneself for the sake of others, it's something you're going to have to try to do. Without this basic bit of knowledge, your Pisces boy could be hurt many times over in his young life by people who will take advantage of his good nature, which might affect his ability to trust. You might want to approach this by allowing Pisces to talk to you about some of the fantasies he has. It's your job to ensure he understands that it's fine to do good deeds, but that it's not smart to foolishly squander his talents for the sake of other people who aren't willing to help him make the world a warmer and more compassionate place.

YOUR PISCES GIRL

Pisces girls are very sweet and feminine. She'll love being dressed in delicate clothing and will adore playing with dolls and pretending to be a princess. Pisces is a classic "little girl" all right, and to some degree it's fine to support her efforts to stay in her protected fantasy world. Yet you'll have to prepare her for being a child and then a woman in the "real" world she will eventually have to face.

Your job is to balance the life of fantasy and frills that she loves to live in with doses of responsibility and reality. It's especially important for her to understand that her generosity has to be allocated, not freely given to whichever person happens to be close enough to receive it. You will almost surely have the experience of watching your child get hurt time and again by people who are only more than happy to take advantage of what she offers, with no intention of giving her anything in return. You can be sympathetic to your Pisces girl, because she'll need you to understand how she feels, but you might also have to ask her what lesson she might have learned. Try to impress upon her how important it is to let people prove themselves, and to avoid giving them everything she has before they have earned her trust or at least shown signs of returning her love, affection, and whatever else Pisces is thinking of giving.

Your Pisces girl will also need to balance her interest in the arts with some grounding activities. Dancing is nice, but so is language and grammar. Poetry would be a great way to introduce her to the concept of using words to express her romantic and creative impulses. She could also benefit from learning martial arts or horseback riding, where she would be forced to focus and concentrate more than she would tend to on her own. On a daily basis, you can reward her for the attempts she makes at organizing her activities and making her life ever more purposeful. When she grows up, she will be very intent on leaving a legacy of love and care for humankind, and it's your job to help her direct her talents and awaken her passions.

TALENTS AND AFFINITIES

ART AND MUSIC

Pisces's special connection with the world beyond the material plane gives your child an extra helping of creative talent. It's important to give Pisces this place to put her dreams and fantasies. If you listen to the music your child plays or look deeply into the little pictures she makes, you'll be able to discover what your Pisces is feeling and help her process her fears and share her triumphs.

LANGUAGE

Pisces likes the idea of self-expression, but doesn't always like to do it according to grammatical and spelling rules. "Fun" and "Phonics" don't go in the same sentence for this whimsical child. Pisces responds more swiftly to learning in the whole-language way, where he can see the entire picture of language at work, and will somehow, if not with perfection, decode the patterns and put it all together to express his ideas and share his thoughts.

MATHEMATICS

Although you'll hear that Pisces isn't very capable of dealing with details, when it comes to higher mathematics Pisces is the one sun sign capable of suspending disbelief long enough to comprehend the intangible world this area of study is made of. Are you skeptical of your dreamy little one's ability to focus on mathematical constructs? Consider this: Albert Einstein was a Pisces.

FAVORITE THINGS

SING THESE SONGS WITH YOUR PISCES CHILD

> **"Row, Row, Row Your Boat":** Life *is* but a dream, after all.

> **"Catch a Wave":** Appeal to your Pisces's King Neptune complex—sittin' on top of the world.

> **"Baby Beluga":** A lovable sea creature personified in a sweet song.

WATCH MOVIES LIKE THIS WITH YOUR PISCES CHILD

> *The Little Mermaid:* Boys and girls will love the characters and the catchy tunes.

> *Free Willy:* Pisces will be delighted to see how it's possible to trust others to help get you out of a jam.

> *The Pagemaster:* Proof to Pisces that it's possible to use imagination and fantasy to overcome fear.

PLAY THESE GAMES WITH YOUR PISCES CHILD

> **Kick the Can:** Give Pisces a sense of power in her feet.

> **Water Polo:** Pisces will love swimming like a fish and scoring simultaneously.

> **Shadow Tag:** A kinder, gentler tag, where you "touch" the other kids' shadows.

READ THESE BOOKS, RHYMES, AND FAIRY TALES TO YOUR PISCES CHILD

> *The Water-Babies:* Covers many of Pisces's big issues, including spirituality and transformation.

> **"Hey Diddle Diddle":** Can you get any more imaginative? Pisces will try!

> **"The Hut in the Forest":** Being nice can be very, very smart.

TREAT YOUR PISCES CHILD TO THESE FOODS

> **Fish:** Soft, not too strong, and very nutritious.

> **Milk:** Help Pisces build those bones—calcium can come from almonds, soy, rice, and coconut, too!

> **Sweet Potatoes:** Pisces will enjoy this tasty and vitamin-rich veggie.

✳ LITTLE CHALLENGES ✳

Raising a Pisces doesn't require a lot of physical strain or interpersonal stress, but it still has its moments of frustration. Most of these will come from Pisces's refusal to join the rest of the world 100 percent of the time. You will swear you told your child something, such as to get ready for school or to pick up a toy you just tripped on, yet Pisces will look at you as though she has no idea what you're talking about.

The Pisces child's mind simply doesn't work the same way yours might. Your little fish is literally swimming in circles through her own little world, and at times your voice may sound like outside static. Pisces kind of knows she should be listening, but the draw of her inner world is just too enticing.

This can be humorous or mildly irritating in most instances, but it can also be dangerous, particularly when Pisces's physical well-being is at risk. Pisces loves the water and must always be watched extra closely whenever there's a chance of your little fish wandering into a pond, pool, lake, or ocean without close supervision. You also must make intense and pointed efforts to wake Pisces out of her dream world and deal with reality, no matter how much you know you're spoiling the party.

✳ DISCIPLINE ✳

Keeping little Pisces in line is easy most of the time. There is very little this child will do that deliberately goes against the rules, but there will be times when your little one just can't resist touching or going somewhere that is not going to do him any real good. In order to teach Pisces how to behave better, you must first communicate and make sure you have established contact with your little Pisces's rational mind. To do this, you might have to sometimes remove all toys, videos, and other distractions and look right into Pisces's eyes when you give instructions.

When Pisces does do things that must be corrected or reprimanded, you have to avoid becoming too harsh. If, for any reason, Pisces becomes afraid of you and what you're doing to correct his behavior, he will simply retreat more into his own little world. Keep the lines of communication open and allow your fish to explain why he makes certain choices. As your little Pisces gets older and more independent, there might be a little bit of deliberate story-telling, where Pisces would have you believe he was doing his homework rather than playing with his army of knights and their elaborate gear.

✳ PISCES'S BABY STYLE ✳

You can dress your Pisces child as a superhero, a fairy, or anything she wants to be, and this little creative sweetie of a child will be as happy as you can imagine. Shoes will be big with Pisces, who need extra support for their feet.

GIRLS: Yes! Pisces will actually enjoy wearing those frilly little things you've been saving and coveting as you imagined what you'd put on your gentle, sweet, and fragile little girl.

BOYS: Pisces boys will love that boho look—expect him to be attracted to a certain hat or shirt that looks somewhat tattered, yet entirely fashionable.

PISCES'S ENVIRONMENT

The Pisces psyche is extremely fragile so make sure it's nice and quiet in your baby's nursery, especially in the first days and weeks; Pisces always needs to have solid sleep times and opportunities to dream. Colors should be soft, even for boys, and there should be some draperies or wall hangings that flow and blow when the wind whispers through the room.

CALMING PISCES

Pisces babies tend to cry a lot, because in many ways they are in a state of shock just from being on planet Earth. Your little Pisces will respond well to being swaddled and held tightly in your arms, and needs as much bodily contact as you can give him. A rocking chair or glider could be your best friend, and you can use it to trick Pisces into believing he is right back in the womb.

The other smart way to calm Pisces down is by giving him a bath. Even if he starts out screaming, being gently washed in warm, clear water will bring your baby back to his element and make him feel soothed and safe. If you have the opportunity to take Pisces near a large body of water, this will help as well. As always, be sure your little fish isn't allowed to get too close to it without your watchful eyes being right there with him. Pisces's attraction to the water outweighs his fear of what might happen upon diving right in.

✶ STIMULATING PISCES ✶

Pisces always needs sounds and signals to bring attention to the real world. Some toys might be too noisy for little fishes' liking, but do try these:

- **A Toy Piano:** Pisces will enjoy the ability to make noise and create tunes and rhythms with very little effort.
- **Bath Toys:** Pisces will stay in the bath for hours, but toys that allow him to stack, squirt, and spray will make bath time even more delightful.
- **Interactive Stories and Movies:** Pisces gets lost so easily in the world of video entertainment, it can be frightening. Keep your child's conscious mind awake by pushing her to add characters and create happy endings with these technically tempting toys.

✶ PISCES'S LEARNING STYLE ✶

Pisces learns almost through osmosis. She isn't the kind who likes to be pushed into flash cards and learning software, but can probably benefit from some form of this kind of home learning anyway. Remember, your Pisces child needs to learn that it's a basic requirement of life to come into the same frame of reference the rest of the world lives in. Concrete teaching of basics like ABCs and 123s will give your Pisces child an introduction to school life that you won't regret taking the time to offer.

PARENTING PISCES

If your sign is . . .

ARIES

You'll think your little fish is pretty adorable! You'll want to rock and bounce the baby, and teach her to walk and run as soon as possible—but you might find that your little fish will need to go just a little bit slower! Your baby Pisces may cry if she is jarred and will need to be coaxed gently into physical activity.

You may notice how frail your child's little body can be. This is because Pisces needs a long time to develop the solid parts of the body. However, you can help your flexible little fish build up her bones and add muscle to her frame. Give Pisces lots of exercise, maybe by allowing her to stand and push off your legs. Rather than coming to the rescue when your Pisces child shows weakness or helplessness, encourage her to learn how to pull up or crawl all on her own. This is the only way that Pisces is truly going to develop her own way of moving through the world. Although your little Pisces may never be a great runner or ballplayer, you might find yourself cheering from the sidelines for your speedy little swimmer.

TAURUS

You and Pisces will get along well from the moment you see one another. You both have a quiet, easygoing way about you, and you'll enjoy watching how easily and completely your baby will relax the minute you pick him up. As your little fish gets older, though, you'll have to struggle to find some common ground.

You, the most practical person in the universe, must find ways to relate to a child who would love to have the privilege of never having to face reality. You might also puzzle over the way Pisces doesn't seem to be impressed by getting new toys or collecting possessions that add to his material assets. There won't be a moment when you don't love your child, of course, but you'll certainly wonder at times how he's going to make it in the real world. You're the perfect teacher for this, of course, so don't be afraid to confront your child with this requirement. For example, don't just give an allowance to Pisces; make him work for it. Doing dishes or learning to run the washing machine at an early age will help ground Pisces and teach how important it is to put one's best foot forward and pay for one's own ticket.

GEMINI

Your Pisces child is a true gift, and you will love playing with this little fish. Pisces will show you how to communicate without words when you first look into those endless eyes and come to grips with the world of wonder that exists behind them. Pisces will look to you to learn how to function in the world and will appreciate your efforts to share information. Yet, Pisces won't always believe the things you think are important are major priorities.

You'll always appreciate your Pisces child's ability to express feelings and thoughts through the arts and you may also want to share in these activities. Yet, you also must accept that he will want to be alone at least some of the time, and allow him to follow the call to that world of imagination that enriches him so fully. You'll enjoy telling your friends about how magical and mystical you find your little fish to be—and you might also learn how valuable it is to explore the world beyond the superficial pleasantries and address those emotions you feel while you look deeply into your little Pisces's eyes.

CANCER

You'll feel from the beginning of your Pisces child's life that you finally have someone in your family who truly understands you. It's true that your little fish is at least as emotionally attuned as you are, but despite your similarities there are some distinctions, too.

Pisces is a little more detached from the day-to-day world than you are. While you're tending to the needs of the people who surround you, Pisces is hoping that you'll do that so she can stay in her own little world without being interrupted! It will be your job to tend to Pisces, but it will also be important for you to teach Pisces the art of caring for oneself. With this ability, your child will be able to master the art of living and live up to his own little life mission, which usually has to do with pointing out the existence of a life beyond "normal" reality and inviting the rest of you to come and join the magical, mystical party.

LEO

Your Pisces baby might seem helpless when you first hold this bundle of spiritual intensity in your arms, but in fact this child has powers beyond any you might imagine. They're not the kind of thing you would perceive as "strength," but when you get to know your little one, you'll discover he knows secrets about life—such as the beauty of learning and connecting with one's spiritual core—that bring a new meaning to yours.

It's very important, while you inspire your child with your own courage and leadership, to also allow Pisces to develop a spiritual connection. This might be through organized religion or through other practices. Even some quiet time, once or twice a day, where you both remain silent and contemplative would be of help to Pisces.

When you give this child, who does have a tendency to space out, a place to put all that otherworldly energy, you have a better chance of bringing him back down to earth when it's time to take a bath or get ready for school on time. You might also learn that you can gain the strength you need in your daily life by connecting with your inner strength from your dreamy, little Pisces!

VIRGO

You'll love your Pisces more than anything else in the world, but there will be certain things about your little fish that you may find hard to accept. For example, your child wasn't born with the instant skills for organization that you have. Instead, Pisces just sort of drifts from one activity to the next, without much concern for finishing what was begun or cleaning up the mess he might have left behind. Things just "call" to your Pisces, as though there were little voices responsible for managing and directing his activities. Unfortunately, these "voices" won't tell your child how to put things in the right order or help you make sense of his choices.

That's where you come in. You'll get along so well with your child as long as you teach him how to be neat and orderly—but you cannot force your little Pisces to be like you. Offer opportunities, insist on certain standards, but never quash Pisces's desire to transcend reality. Instead, show your child how much you love him by taking the time to at least visit the world of wonder he finds within.

LIBRA

You'll love having this Pisces child in your life and will enjoy watching her learn and grow. The two of you will have a lot of things in common—including a love for the arts—but your appreciation will come from two different places. While you can see the value in beauty and aesthetics, Pisces lives in that fantasy world that creates art, music, drama, and poetry.

Try to inspire your Pisces child by offering opportunities to create. Provide crayons, finger paints, and spaces that don't have to be kept pristine for Pisces to experiment in. Take her to the museum, to concerts, or to plays directed at children; after all, stimulating your child's imagination will only help it to grow. Just make sure it isn't the only thing that little Pisces does with his time.

It's also important for Pisces to learn how to be on time for appointments and to comply with the regimentation of school. Put some patterns of order into Pisces's life; maybe these schedules will help you learn to be more speedy and sure about making your decisions.

SCORPIO

You'll feel a true affinity to your Pisces child that goes way beyond the usual bonds of the parent-child relationship. There's a very deep quality to your little fish that reminds you to check in with your own connection to the world of imagination and infinite love that exists behind the illusion of the material world.

Your little fish will astound you with the simplicity of her observations and the profound nature of her statements. You might at times wonder whether you're guiding your child through her life or if she's teaching and helping you through yours. Ideally, it will be a little bit of both.

Give Pisces structure by setting goals for her and by giving her the skill sets she needs to achieve them. You may have to spend more time teaching your little fish how to accomplish physical tasks than you would with other children, but don't worry. Pisces will learn, usually from watching you and coming to understand how important it is to not only do well, but to be excellent.

SAGITTARIUS

The Pisces baby will seem like a china doll when you first hold her in your arms. It's true that you might have very different ways of seeing the world, and the delicate and easygoing style of Pisces's nature will be a marvel in and of itself. The challenge for you will come when you realize how important it is to be gentle and soft with this child. You're not usually in this frame of mind but you can easily adapt and learn a less energetic touch.

Don't let your little fish's sensitivity keep you from performing necessary tasks, from changing a diaper to removing a Band-Aid from a sore finger or foot. Your Pisces will always object to being hurt because the psychic impulses are so intense with this little soul. Still, you have to teach her how to live in her body and how to take care of it, too. You can introduce your little Pisces to exercise, and even if she doesn't want to try it at first, eventually that will change. One day you'll probably be rolling up your mats and sauntering off to a parent-child yoga class together.

CAPRICORN

The Pisces child is very different than someone with your sign, but in so many ways you're the perfect parent for this delicate little soul. While Pisces tends to spend way too much time in the world of fantasy, you tend to spend too much time worrying about your position in the material world. As soon as you get to know this little fish, you may begin to see how the two of you can learn from each other and become better people when you integrate both worlds into your respective life experiences.

Pisces doesn't have the kind of ambition you do, but he is very capable of becoming a success. You can teach the importance of mastering skills and competing to win your position, and to some degree Pisces will follow. Still, your child won't really believe that winning could matter more than being happy and gratified by the activity. This is why, while you might want your child to be an accountant, he's more likely to end up becoming a brilliant math professor. No matter what your little fish grows up to be, you'll be so proud either way.

AQUARIUS

The moment you pick up your Pisces child you'll need to remember the words "live and let live." Pisces has a tremendous capacity for learning, but your little fish won't have the same desires and ambitions you do. Funny enough, though, the two of you do share the desire for all of humanity to live in peace and harmony. You take a more material view toward this wish, while your Pisces baby will manifest it more in a spiritual sense.

If you're open to the idea of being "taught" by your little one, you can learn all you'll ever need to know simply by looking into his eyes. There's a sense that little Pisces knows every secret in the universe and will share it with you—as long as you'll listen and observe. That's where the hard part comes. Try to avoid imposing your beliefs on Pisces and don't insist he follow practices that are really your own personal preferences. It's far more important that Pisces learns how to develop his own tastes, and your child never will if he is told what to like. The biggest challenge here for you will be to give this child space, and when you do you'll watch a most marvelous being unfold right before your eyes. This alone could be the greatest gift you give to the world.

PISCES

You have a child that's a Pisces, just like you! With any luck, you've learned enough about yourself by now to help this little creature avoid some of the mistakes you've made. But for now, maybe all you need to do is hold your little one close and feel the way your hearts meet on the same wavelength.

You're going to have to work hard to teach Pisces about the "real" world. Although you're not the most organized or structured person, you can show Pisces the utility of putting things in their places and learning language so she can express her thoughts, feelings, and needs to others in a way they'll understand.

Most of all, you'll need to teach Pisces how and when to trust. Your child will begin by learning to trust you, so be strong and dependable but don't let your whimsical side wither either; allow your own imagination to contribute to the exposure you give your child to the arts, music, and the life lessons that can be conveyed through fairy tales. If you handle all these things the right way, you'll prove just how capable you Pisces people are of fostering the spirit and allowing it to grow in ways that will ultimately be a great service to humanity.

Afterword

Congratulations! Now that you know what the stars have written for your loving relationship with your little one, you're well prepared to parent your child in an insightful and personal way. Your child looks to you to set an example for how he should behave, what is important, and what kind of person he should grow up to be. Now you know how to personalize your parenting and nurture the person that your little one will become.

But as much as you have to teach your artistic little Libra or your young, ambitious Capricorn, your child has a lot of lessons to give you too! Your child will teach you how to be patient, more sensitive, or perhaps more structured or rigid. You'll learn how to set boundaries and when to let your barriers down so your child can feel the deep love and watchful protection you have to offer. Moments you may never have imagined will come when your children mirror the kind of love and support you offer them—and realize that you've definitely been doing something right!

The process of watching your children and their personalities unfold is a sweet gift, and—with the insight of astrology—you're able to get a more conscious grasp on that miracle. The ultimate goal of knowing and using astrology is to become aware of who you are, so you can work on evolving for your entire life—and now you know how to help your child do it, too.

From the day your baby came into your life, you were forever changed in a fundamental way. The dance that goes on between you and your little one over the years—the giving and taking, the laughing and loving, and the bond that will last throughout your entire life—has been going on for eons, certainly ever since humankind first looked skyward and observed the stars and the planets. Use this ancient science to help your child live, grow, and love in the best way possible: with you by his side.

Index

About the Author

JUDI VITALE currently provides research for *Marie Claire*, and writes horoscopes and articles for ReadTheStars.com, Tarot.com, dailyhoroscope.com, *Glitter* magazine, and on Dr. Laura Berman's website (*www.drlauraberman.com*). She is certified as an astrologer by NCGR Professional Astrologers' Alliance. After thirty years in New York City, she now resides near Pittsburgh, PA.

BEYOND HERE

Sure, this world is fascinating, but
what's beyond is even more intriguing...

Want a place to share stories and experiences about all things strange and unusual? From UFOs and apparitions to dream interpretation, the Tarot, astrology, and more, the **BEYOND HERE** blog is the newest hot spot for paranormal activity!

Sign up for our newsletter at
www.adamsmedia.com/blog/paranormal
and download our free Haunted U.S. Hot Spots Map!